OTHER BOOKS BY SCOTT HAHN

The Lamb's Supper:
The Mass as Heaven on Earth
(Doubleday)

Hail Holy Queen:
The Mother of God in the Word of God
(Doubleday)

First Comes Love:
Finding Your Family in the Church and the Trinity
(Doubleday)

A Father Who Keeps His Promises:
God's Covenant Love in Scripture
(Servant Books)

Understanding "Our Father":
Biblical Reflections on the Lord's Prayer
(Emmaus Road Publishing)

Rome Sweet Home:
Our Journey to Catholicism
(Ignatius Press)

Catholic for a Reason:
Scripture and the Mystery of the Family of God
(Emmaus Road Publishing)

For a catalog of over 500 titles of Scott Hahn's talks on tape (or CD),
contact Saint Joseph Communications in West Covina, CA
(Phone: 1–800–526–2151, Online: www.saintjoe.com)

LORD, HAVE MERCY

The Healing Power of Confession

SCOTT HAHN

DOUBLEDAY
New York • London • Toronto • Sydney • Auckland

PUBLISHED BY DOUBLEDAY
A division of Random House, Inc.

DOUBLEDAY and the portrayal of an anchor with a dolphin are
registered trademarks of Random House, Inc.

Library of Congress Cataloging-in-Publication Data
Hahn, Scott.
Lord, have mercy : the healing power of confession / by Scott
Hahn.—1st ed.
p.   cm.
Includes bibliographical references.
1. Penance. I. Title.
BX2260 .H15 2003
234'.166—dc21   2002041219

Nihil Obstat: Reverend James Dunfee, Censor Librorum
Imprimatur: Most Reverend Robert Daniel Conlon, Bishop of
Steubenville, December 18, 2002

ISBN 0-385-50170-6
PRINTED IN THE UNITED STATES OF AMERICA

April 2003

First Edition

1 3 5 7 9 10 8 6 4 2

To Gabriel Kirk Hahn:

Omnia in bonum (Rom 8:28)

CONTENTS

CHAPTER 1

GETTING OUR
STORIES STRAIGHT

CONFESSION IS A mixed-up matter for many Catholics. The more we need it, the less we seem to want it. The more we choose to sin, the less we want to discuss our sins.

It's only natural, this reluctance to speak up about our moral failures. If you're the losing pitcher in the final game of the World Series, you're not going to seek out the sportswriters on your way to the locker room. If your mismanagement of the family business has driven most of your kin to bankruptcy court, you probably won't volunteer that information at a cocktail party.

Sin, moreover, is the one thing in life we *should* be ashamed about. For sin is a transgression against almighty God, which is a more serious matter than a business blunder or a fat pitch down the middle of the plate. When we sin, we reject the love of God, to some degree, and nothing can be hid from God.

Raised from the Dread

So, again, it's only *natural* for us to wince at the very thought of kneeling before God's representatives on earth, his priests, and of speaking our sins aloud—in clear terms, without whitewash, without excuses. Self-accusation has never been humanity's favorite pastime. Yet it's essential to every confession.

To dread confession is only natural, yes, but nothing that's "only natural" can get us to heaven, or even win us happiness here on earth. Heaven is supernatural; it's above the natural, and every *natural* happiness is fleeting. Our natural instincts tell us to avoid pain and embrace pleasure, but the wisdom of the ages tells us things like "No pain, no gain."

Whatever we suffer from speaking our sins aloud, it's far less than the pain we bring on ourselves by living in inward or outward denial, acting as if our sins don't exist or don't matter. "If we say we are without sin," the Bible tells us, "we deceive ourselves" (1 Jn 1:8).

Self-deception is a nasty thing in itself, but it's only the beginning of our troubles. For when we begin to deny our sins, we begin to live a lie. In our speech or in our thought, we have broken important connections of cause and effect, because we have denied our own responsibility for our own most grievous faults. Once we've done this, even in a small matter, we have begun to erode the contours of reality. We can't quite get our story straight, and this can't help but affect our lives, our health, and our relationships—most directly and most profoundly, our relationship with God.

3

That's a big claim, I know, and some people might think I'm exaggerating. The rest of the book, I pray, will bear this lesson out. It's a lesson I began to learn, the hard way, long before I believed in God or saw a confessional.

Pittsburgh Stealer

I have a confession to make. In my early teens, I ran with the sort of crowd that is every parent's nightmare. We did some minor mischief before moving on to petty crime. For a while, shoplifting at the mall was our Saturday afternoon pastime. One day, I got caught stealing record albums. I won't tire you with the details just now. I'll only say that I was more skillful as a liar than as a thief.

Two store detectives, both middle-aged women, hauled me off to the department store's interrogation room. I must have looked pitiful. I was the smallest kid in my eighth-grade class. I was thirteen, but I looked about ten. One of the detectives looked at me and said, "You look too young to steal. . . . Did you steal those albums for yourself?"

She didn't know it, but with those words she had given me my alibi. Working from her mere suggestion, I fabricated a story about how a group of local kids—known delinquents and drug users—threatened to beat up my friend and me unless we stole albums for them.

The interrogator's face flushed with a motherly indignation. "How could they do such a thing? Why didn't you tell your mom?"

"I was afraid," I said meekly.

A Pittsburgh police officer soon arrived, and in short order I managed—with the store detectives' help!—to persuade them that the real guilt lay elsewhere than with me. The police, in turn, helped me to make the case convincingly for my mother.

Scott-Free

Soon I was, literally, home-free. When Mom parked the car in our driveway, I mumbled something about being tired. She was sympathetic. I went directly to my room and closed the door.

Immediately I heard muffled conversation from downstairs. I couldn't make out words, but I knew that the soft voice was my mother's and that the voice gradually rising in volume and pitch was my dad's. This didn't bode well.

Soon the sound of heavy feet came padding up the steps and then down the hall to my room. I felt more than heard the knock at the door.

It was Dad, of course, and I let him in.

He fixed his eyes on mine, which immediately shifted to a distant point on the carpet.

"Your mother told me what happened today."

I nodded.

He kept staring at me. "You were *made* to steal those record albums?"

"Yeah."

He looked at me hard and repeated, "You were *made* to steal records?"

As I nodded again in reply, I could see his eyes shift toward the towering stack of records beside my stereo.

He looked back toward me. "And where'd you drop the records off, after you stole them?"

"At a tree stump," I replied, "in the woods near the mall."

"Can you show me that tree stump?"

I nodded again.

"Okay," he said. "Get on your coat, Scottie. Let's go for a walk."

Forest Clump

The woods were about three hundred yards from our house, and the mall was about a half-mile walk through the woods. The foliage was thick, so I was sure I'd see lots of tree stumps. All I'd have to do is choose one.

Sure enough, as we walked, I saw plenty of of trees, plenty of leaves, plenty of twigs, even some fallen branches—but a conspicuous absence of stumps. My dad had let me lead, so he couldn't see my eyes scanning from side to side, with increasing desperation. I felt a certain panic when I saw the clearing ahead. The woods were ending, and I hadn't seen a stump.

At the very edge of the woods, with the mall straight in front of us, I said, "Over there. That's where the guys were sniffing glue."

"OK," Dad replied, "where's the stump?"

"It's that big mound of dirt over there. That clump."

He looked right back at me. "You said tree stump."

I squirmed. "Well, clump, stump . . ."

"Clump . . . stump," he repeated, pausing painfully between the words. I was expecting his temper to explode, for him to turn around in a rage and call me a liar—but all he said was, "Let's go home."

In the eternity it took us to walk through the woods, my father never said a word. I found myself no longer dreading the explosion, but almost longing for it. His silence was killing me.

We got home. He closed the door. He took off his jacket, took off his shoes, went upstairs.

In a moment, I, too, went upstairs, into my room alone, and closed my door. You'd think that I'd be celebrating a victory. I had managed to keep my crooked story straight enough to fool two store detectives, a town policeman, and my mother! But I was celebrating nothing. I was experiencing a whole new thing. It was at that moment that I began to realize what it meant to have a human heart. I felt such an overwhelming sense of shame because my dad didn't believe my story, because he knew the boy he loved had lied and stolen.

What happened to me was not merely the awakening of a conscience. It was the discovery of a relationship. I had always seen this man in my life as judge, jury, and executioner. Whenever I had done something wrong, I feared getting caught, standing trial, and being punished. But that day, I discovered there was something worse than inciting Dad's wrath, and it was breaking Dad's heart. I had done this, and I hated it.

Setting the Records Straight

My father was not what anyone would call a devout believer. He wasn't even sure that he believed in God. But I would gradually discern, over the course of years, that at that lonely moment when I was thirteen, my dad represented God's fatherhood to me, and he began to set my story straight. I was no longer reveling in my "successful" lies or thefts. I was exposed in my guilt; I was ashamed of myself and more alone than I had ever been before.

I wish I could say that this was the moment of my conversion to Christ—a dazzling and sudden miracle, like Saint Paul's encounter with Jesus on the road to Damascus—but that wasn't the case. Still, it was an awakening, a beginning.

My juvenile delinquency sets me apart, perhaps, from most people in their youth. Yet in the making of alibis, I am surely not alone. We've all done it, in every generation since Adam and Eve. Sometimes we do it in small ways, sometimes in bigger ways. We do it in our everyday conversation and in our private reveries. When we tell the tales of our troubles— at work or at home—do we include the details that might cast a shadow on our own responsibility in the matter? Or do we instead portray ourselves as either the hero or the helpless victim in an ongoing office or domestic drama? If you and I think hard about the way we talk about the events of daily life, we'll probably find instances in which we exaggerate our victimhood and magnify the faults of others, even as we ignore our own. We find excuses and mitigating circumstances for all our own blunders; yet we're fairly merciless in recounting those of our neighbors or coworkers. Often, our friends and family members will believe our side of the story. Often, we will begin to believe it ourselves.

All of this, some people will tell you, is—like the aversion to confession—"only natural." But that's not true. It's not natural at all. To falsify facts is actually to destroy nature. It destroys things-as-they-are, along with nature's delicate web of cause and effect, and replaces them with things-as-we-wish-they-were: castles in the air.

Forgotten, Not Forgiven

One of my favorite philosophers, Josef Pieper, wrote that this "falsification of memory" is among our greatest enemies, for it strikes "at the deepest root" of our spiritual and moral lives. "There is no more insidious way for error to establish itself than by this falsification of the memory through slight retouches, displacements, discolorations, omissions, shifts of accent."

Once we do this—and we all do—we begin to lose the true narrative thread in our lives. Things no longer make sense to us. Relationships grow cold. We lose our sense of purpose and our sense of ourselves.

I'll say it again: This is something we all do, though we must never think it is natural. Thus, those symptoms of unease are, perhaps, just as familiar to us all. How, then, can we overcome this malaise, when it's pandemic and yet so subtle that it eludes diagnosis? Even Josef Pieper found the task daunting. "The peril," he said, "is the greater for its being so imperceptible. . . . Nor can such falsification be quickly detected by the probing conscience, even when it applies itself to this task. The honesty of memory can be ensured only by a rectitude of the whole human being."

That's a tall order. It is, however, achievable, as we can see in the lives of the saints. What's more, such total rectitude is what God has asked of each and every one of us. "Be perfect," Jesus said, "as your heavenly Father is perfect" (Mt 5:48). If God has commanded this, He will certainly give us the power to carry it out. Moreover, in that brief command, He even revealed the source of our power: It is the fatherhood of God. "Be perfect . . . as your Father."

If in my teen years I had spent all my time in the sight of my earthly father, I would never have shoplifted; I certainly would never have lied to my dad.

Yet God is our Father, and we live every moment in His sight; and still we sin. We act like toddler children who think that Mom can't see them as long as they can't see Mom. So they turn their back to Mom and reach for the forbidden cookies.

We live always in the presence of our Father, who wishes us to be perfect. If our earthly fathers wish us to complete a task, they will make sure we have all that we need to do so. Our heavenly Father—Who owns all and is all-powerful—will surely do the same.

What is essential is that we recognize His constant presence, so that we realize we are always, in a sense, under judgment. Yet God does not preside in our lives like a magistrate in a court. He judges as a father judges, with love. That's a double-edged sword, of course, because fathers will demand more from their children than a judge will demand from the accused; but fathers will also show greater mercy.

The Road Most Traveled

We long to know peace in our Father's arms; yet something dark within us tells us that it's easier to turn our back to Him. We long to live in the truth, with no secrets to cover up and no lies to protect; yet something dark within us tells us that our sins are best left unspoken.

"There is a way which seems right to a man," says the Bible's wise king, "but its end is the way to death" (Prv 14:12). How can we know this dead-end road when we see it? We can be sure that it is any road—no matter how right it seems at the time—that would lead us away from confessing our sins to God, in the way that He wishes. Sad to say, our ancestors walked such a road, almost from the beginning of their earthly journey.

CHAPTER 2

ACTS OF CONTRITION:
THE DEEPEST ROOTS
OF PENANCE

MANY PEOPLE THINK of confession as something that was introduced by the Catholic Church. That's true, in a sense, because confession is a sacrament of the New Covenant, and so it could not be established until Jesus sealed that covenant with His blood (Mt 26:27). But in the tradition of Israel, to which Jesus was faithful, the enactment of the covenant always contained provisions for the remission of sins.

Confession, then, was new; but only in the sense that a blossom is new. It was present almost from the beginning of time—as a flower is in its seeds and shoots and buds—and appears on many pages of the Old Testament. For as long as sin has been in the world, so have confession, penance, and reconciliation.

Open your Bible, start at the beginning, and you need not go far before you encounter the first foreshadowings of the confessional. In fact, you find them with original sin, the first sin of the first man and woman.

The Naked Truth

Adam and Eve had sinned. Right now, we need not go into the nature of their sin. (We'll study that, in depth, in a later chapter.) If all we knew of their sin was that they had disobeyed the Lord God, that would be enough. He was their Creator; He was their Father; and they had violated His only commandment: "You may freely eat of every tree of the garden; but of the tree of the knowledge of good and evil you shall not eat, for in the day that you eat of it you shall die" (Gen 2:16–17).

Tempted by a deadly serpent, they touched and they ate—and immediately they knew that everything had changed. Suddenly, they were ashamed of their nakedness. Suddenly, they were afraid. "And they heard the sound of the Lord God walking in the garden in the cool of the day, and the man and his wife hid themselves from the presence of the Lord God among the trees of the garden" (Gen 3:8). This is the behavior I spoke about in the last chapter. They duck behind the bushes, as if they could hide themselves from an all-knowing, all-seeing, and loving Father.

What does God do then? You and I might expect Him to thunder, "I saw that!" from the heavens. But He doesn't. Instead, He plays along with Adam and Eve's deception. God calls out to Adam: "Where are you?" (Gen 3:9)—as if He needed to be informed of anyone's whereabouts!

Adam replies with an evasive statement: "I heard the sound of You in the garden, and I was afraid, because I was naked; and I hid myself" (Gen 3:10). Remarkable: In just a few words, he manages to express fear, shame, defensiveness, self-pity—but not contrition. In fact, he seems to be shifting the blame toward God, Whose power Adam suddenly finds intimidating.

God again responds with a question: "Who told you that you were naked? Have you eaten of the tree of which I commanded you not to eat?" (Gen 3:11).

Adam doesn't hesitate to place the blame squarely on his wife. "The woman whom You gave to be with me, she gave me fruit of the tree, and I ate" (Gen 3:12).

God still pronounces no judgment, but asks yet another question, this time directed to the woman: "What is this that you have done?" (Gen 3:13).

Almighty God has asked four questions in four short verses. What is He doing here? If God knows everything, then He already knows the answer to each of those questions, and He knows it better than this self-deluded and serpent-deluded couple. What does God want from them?

It's clear, from the text, that He wants them to confess their sin with true sorrow. He begins with open-ended questions that gently invite an explanation; He proceeds to get more specific, until, at last, He asks the woman point-blank what she has done. Through it all, however—from coaxing to interrogation—no confession emerges. Rather than take responsibility for his action, Adam first blames his helpmate and then blames God: "*You* gave me this woman, and she gave me the fruit!"

As I said at the beginning of the last chapter: The more we need confession, the less we seem to want it. It was as true for Adam and Eve as for all their descendants in the human race.

Cain's Not Able

Consider only their immediate descendant, their firstborn son, Cain.

Cain, out of envy, commits the world's first murder. No sooner does the murderer finish off his victim, his brother Abel, than God says to Cain: "Where is Abel your brother?" (Gen 4:9).

Again, God is not seeking information. He does not need to be informed about Abel's whereabouts. He is, rather, giving Cain an opportunity to confess his sin.

Cain, however, doesn't take the Lord up on His offer. He lies instead. Where is his brother Abel? "I do not know," Cain replies. "Am I my brother's keeper?"

Once more, God does not accuse Cain, but invites him to confess, even presenting him with the evidence of his crime: "What have you done? The voice of your brother's blood is crying to Me from the ground" (Gen 4:10).

To the end of the episode, however, Cain remains unrepentant, his sin unconfessed. Rather than acknowledge that he has made a victim of Abel, Cain blames God for victimizing Cain! When he complains, "My punishment is greater than I can bear" (Gen 4:13), he isn't just saying "woe is me"; he's saying "unjust are You" to God, his judge. Rather than confessing his own injustice, Cain accuses God of injustice. He goes on, then, to castigate God for taking away his joy and his means of making a living: "Behold, You have driven me this day from the ground; and from Your face I shall be hidden" (Gen 4:14). Indeed, Cain goes so far as to accuse God of betraying him to a world full of murderers: "I shall be a fugitive and a wanderer on the earth, and whoever finds me will slay me" (Gen 4:14).

It doesn't take a psychiatrist to see what's going on here. Cain is assuming Abel's victim status and projecting his own guilt onto God. "Now I can't work. Now I can't fellowship with You. Now I have to suffer injustice." Moreover, he's accusing the rest of humanity of murderous intent, when he himself is, so far, history's only murderer. Like his parents, Cain can muster a range of emotions—fear, shame, defensiveness, self-pity—but he won't say he's sorry. He refuses to acknowledge his sin.

Repent or Resent

Cain's behavior might seem familiar to us. All these centuries later, men and women are no more eager to own up to their failings. And the pattern of evasion is no different. People who won't repent will come to resent. Those who refuse to accuse themselves will find outlandish ways to excuse themselves. They—we—will blame our circumstances, limitations, heredity, environment. Ultimately, however, when we do this, we are following after our first ancestors. We are blaming God and making Him the object of our resentment; because it was He Who created our circumstances, our heredity, and our environment.

The more we choose to sin, the less we want to discuss our sins. The more we need confession, the less we seem to want it. Like Cain and Adam and Eve, we'll talk about almost anything else—causes and consequences, blame and punishment—but not confession.

God Makes It Rite

In the successive covenants—with Noah, Abraham, Moses, and David—God gradually revealed more about Himself and His ways to a greater number of people. If at first the human generations didn't succeed in confessing, God did not weary of inviting them. In fact, in the fine points of the Law of Moses, he gave His people very specific, ritual ways to confess their sins. Some people today dismiss ritual as merely mechanical or mindless actions; but that is simply not true. We humans are dependent on routines; without them, we would not be able to order our days or our lifetimes. From brushing our teeth or locking the doors, to saying "I love you" or taking marriage vows, routine actions—some large and some small—enable us to accomplish the really important work of everyday life.

Many points of the Law concerned themselves with such routines and rituals, and a number of points concerned themselves specifically with the confession of sins. Take, for example, Leviticus 5:5–6, which deals with the various sins people commit when they swear rashly. "When a man is guilty in any of these, he shall confess the sin he has committed, and he shall bring his guilt offering to the Lord for the sin which he has committed, a female from the flock, a lamb or a goat, for a sin offering; and the priest shall make atonement for him for his sin."

By giving His people a clear plan of action, God makes it possible for individuals to confess their sins. First, He explicitly insists upon such a confession. Then, He gives the sinners something to do—a liturgical act of sacrifice and penance. And, finally, He insists that they do all this with the help and the intercession of a priest. All of these elements would survive intact throughout the history of Israel and of the renewed Israel, the Church of Jesus Christ.

We should not underestimate the power of these "acts" of contrition. In the words of a modern saint: Love means deeds, not just sweet words. A popular slogan back in the 1970s was "Love means never having to say you're sorry." But that's not true. Love means not only saying "I'm sorry," but showing it, too. This is human nature—though our fallen nature resists it mightily—and the God Who created our nature knows what works for us. We need to *say* "I'm sorry"; we need to *show* it; and we need to *do* something about it.

God's law recognizes these fine points of human psychology and works with them, first to move His people beyond their resistance to confession, and then to move them beyond liturgical confession to legal satisfaction. "And the Lord said to Moses, 'Say to the people of Israel, When a man or woman commits any of the sins that men commit by breaking faith with the Lord, and that person is guilty, he shall confess his sin which he has committed; and he shall make full restitution for his wrong, adding a fifth to it, and giving it to him to whom he did the wrong' " (Num 5:5–7). (Both the legal and liturgical aspects of confession will figure in our later consideration of the New Covenant sacrament of penance.)

Like faith, sorrow for sins must show itself through works (see Mt 3:8–10 and Jas 2:19, 22, 26). We can see this even in human relationships. When we offend someone, we're often slow to admit our fault. We make excuses; we deny responsibility. But in order to heal the relationship, we need to confess—to say we're sorry—even though we don't *want* to say it. Not only that, we need to "make it up" to the person we've offended. Of course, all this applies, and in a far greater degree, when the one we've offended is the Lord.

A Mess to Confess

God made confession possible by enacting it in law, in Israel's liturgy. We must not, however, underestimate the difficulty of these Old Covenant acts of penance. They may have clarified man's way to repentance, but they did not necessarily make it easy. Only an armchair interpreter would dismiss Israel's confession, sacrifice, and penance as mere ritual. No, these were arduous matters, and they cost something.

Imagine yourself, after recognizing that you have sinned, preparing to make your confession and sacrifice. This could only be done at the Temple in Jerusalem, so you would have to plan your journey—perhaps several days on foot or horse-back—over dusty, rocky roads that were infested with bandits and predatory animals.

Depending on the type of your sin and its gravity, you might have to offer a goat, a sheep, or even a bull. You could bring one with you or, if you had the money, buy one from the merchants in Jerusalem. You would, of course, have to subdue the animal; in the case of a bull, that by itself would be quite demanding. Still, your penance would have only just begun.

Once in Jerusalem, you would lead your beast uphill to the outer court of the Temple. At the inner court, you would tell the reason for your sacrifice. Then, in front of the altar, someone would hand you a knife, and you—yourself—would kill the animal. You yourself would butcher the animal. You would do the cutting and the ripping. You would do the separating of the parts. You would detach the bloody limbs and take out the organs and hand it all, piece by piece, to the priest for burning. You would remove any waste matter from the intestines and purify those parts. You would also sing penitential psalms while the priest caught the animal's blood and sprinkled it over the altar.

All this made up an "act of contrition" that a sinner should never forget. Old Testament scholar Gordon Wenham has described these sacrifices in exhaustive (and exhausting!) detail in his commentaries on Leviticus and Numbers. At the end of it all, he concludes: "Using a little imagination every reader of the Old Testament soon realizes that these ancient sacrifices were very moving occasions. They make modern church services seem tame and dull by comparison. The ancient worshipper did not just listen to the minister and sing a few hymns. He was actively involved in the worship. He had to choose an unblemished animal from his own flock, bring it to the sanctuary, kill it and dismember it with his own hands, then watch it go up in smoke before his very eyes."

When you acted sacrificially in the Old Covenant, it was a deeply personal matter, yet it was also a public matter; it was also humbling and costly. You had to sacrifice cattle; and, in an agrarian culture, that's capital—that's economic power. Let there be no doubt: God called forth from His people godly sorrow for sin and true personal sacrifice.

How often did Israelites have to go through this? Lay people confessed their sins at least once a year during Passover; the priests did so on the Day of Atonement.

Mourning Has Broken

Over time, the people of God developed a rich vocabulary for contrition, confession, and penance, in words and hymns, but also in gestures and actions. Confession, then as now, was not just a spiritual matter; it was something the sinner embodied. It was sometimes something he wore on his flesh. It was an outward sign of an inward reality. It was a sacrament of the Old Covenant. This does not mean it was a mere ritual. Sinners showed their sorrow and their love, not just with sweet words but with deeds that were difficult and bloody; and their deeds, in turn, worked to deepen their sorrow and humility.

Again, these confessions were not merely mental exercises; they were embodied in vivid ways. They were not simply private; they took place in the presence of the Church, the assembly of Israel, or its delegates, the priests.

"And when Ahab heard those words, he rent his clothes, and put sackcloth upon his flesh, and fasted and lay in sackcloth, and went about dejectedly" (1 Kgs 21:27).

"Then David and the elders, clothed in sackcloth, fell upon their faces. And David said to God, 'Was it not I who gave command to [sin by calling for a census]? It is I who have sinned and done very wickedly'" (1 Chr 21:16–17).

"Now . . . the people of Israel were assembled with fasting and in sackcloth, and with earth upon their heads. And the Israelites separated themselves from all foreigners, and stood and confessed their sins and the iniquities of their fathers" (Neh 9:1–2).

Sackcloth and ashes, weeping, falling prostrate upon the ground—these were all common signs of mourning in the ancient world. The Israelites used them, quite spontaneously, to express sorrow for their sins. And the metaphor is perfect, for sin causes a death—a real loss of spiritual life, which is far more deadly than any physical death. Sinners, then, have good reason to mourn.

We modern sinners could learn much from our ancient forebears, as the first Christians most certainly did.

CHAPTER 3

A New Order
in the Court:
The Full Flowering of
the Sacrament

ISRAEL'S ACTS OF contrition were profound and personal. They were surely memorable; and they must have produced a lasting effect in the lives of many people. Thus, when we find Jesus and His apostles speaking of confession and forgiveness, we should keep in mind what these words meant to them, and we should keep vividly in mind the deeds that these words signified.

For we cannot appreciate the New Testament at all if we have no understanding of the Old Testament sacraments. Jesus did not come to replace something bad with something good; He came, rather, to take something already great and holy—something God Himself had already begun—and bring it to a divine fulfillment.

Take the Passover, for example. Ancient Israel's feast marked the night when each family in the people of God sacrificed a lamb so that their firstborn son might be saved from the angel of death (Ex 12). The Passover of the firstborn represents one of the pivotal events in Israel's history; yet it pales when compared to the Passover of Christ, the Lamb of God, Who came to save the entire world. Israel's renewal of its covenant with God took place annually at the feast of Passover. But the Passover of Christ—His suffering, death, and resurrection—is re-presented every day in the Mass.

The Old Covenant did not die out, exhausted and spent, but rather came to new life with the New Covenant of Jesus Christ. In their ancient form, the Old Covenant sacrifices were never enough, and they always pointed to something greater than themselves. God had established them to foreshadow their future fulfillment. They did this, in one way, by hinting at the greatness to come; but, in another, by showing their own inadequacy.

Even with the sacrifices and the ancient sacraments of confession, man fell into sin again and again; and no offering could make up for his offenses against a God infinitely perfect, a Father perfectly loving. The high priest in Jerusalem, says the Letter to the Hebrews, stood every day "offering repeatedly the same sacrifices, which can never take away sins" (Heb 10:11).

The old ways would not do. If sacraments were to take away the sins of the world and the sins of individuals, God Himself would have to administer the sacraments. And so He did.

Lame of God

"To err is human, to forgive divine." Thousands of years before Alexander Pope wrote those words, the principle was a hallmark of Israel's religion. People sinned; and even "the righteous man falls seven times a day" (Prv 24:16). To forgive these sins, however, was the province of God alone. Man's confessions and sacrifices did not obligate God's forgiveness. To err was human; but to forgive was divine, a sovereign act of God.

Thus, when Jesus pronounced forgiveness of sins, we see that He presented people with a dilemma: Either He was usurping an authority that belonged to God, or He was God incarnate. Nowhere is this shown as dramatically as in the story of Jesus' encounter with a paralyzed man, which appears in three of the four gospels.

> He said to the paralytic, "My son, your sins are forgiven." Now some of the scribes were sitting there, questioning in their hearts, "Why does this man speak thus? It is blasphemy! Who can forgive sins but God alone?" And immediately Jesus, perceiving in His spirit that they thus questioned within themselves, said to them, "Why do you question thus in your hearts? Which is easier, to say to the paralytic, 'Your sins are forgiven,' or to say, 'Rise, take up your pallet and walk?' But that you may know that the Son of man has authority on earth to forgive sins"—He said to the paralytic—"I say to you, rise, take up your pallet and go home." (Mk 2:5–11)

"Your sins are forgiven." Jesus, here, is claiming for Himself a power possessed not even by the high priest of the Temple. He is exercising a *divine* prerogative in declaring the total remission of someone's sins. For Jesus, healing the soul was a greater and more divine action than healing the body. Indeed, He performed the latter to signify the former. The healing is an outward sign of the (greater) inward reality.

This is a matter of immense consequence. Those who witnessed Jesus' action knew that they faced a decision: Either they must put faith in His divinity, or they must condemn Him as a blasphemer. The scribes, in their hearts, accused Him of blasphemy. The Church, for her part, called upon Him as God.

Loose Canons

It is a mark of the believer, then, to put faith in Christ's power to forgive sins. Moreover, we must recognize He has chosen to exercise that power in a particular way. On the day He rose from the dead, Jesus appeared to His disciples and said to them, "Peace be with you. As the Father has sent Me, even so I send you." Then He did something curious. He shared with them—the first priests of the New Covenant—His own life and His own power. "And when He had said this, He breathed on them, and said to them, 'Receive the Holy Spirit. If you forgive the sins of any, they are forgiven; if you retain the sins of any, they are retained' " (Jn 20:22–23).

He was establishing them as priests, to administer a sacrament, but also as judges, to pronounce judgment upon the actions of believers. He thus gave them a power exceeding what had formerly belonged to the priests of Israel. The rabbis referred to this ancient priestly power in terms of "binding and loosing," and Jesus used those very words to describe what He was giving to His disciples. For the rabbis, to bind or loose meant to judge someone to be in communion with the chosen people, or cut off from that group's life and worship. According to the rabbis, the priests had the power to reconcile and to excommunicate.

Jesus, though, was not merely transferring authority. In bringing this old office to its fulfillment, He was adding a new dimension. No longer would the authorities pass a sentence that was merely earthly. Since the Church shared the power of God incarnate, her power would extend as far as the power of God. "Truly, I say to you, whatever you bind on earth shall be bound in heaven, and whatever you loose on earth shall be loosed in heaven" (Mt 18:18).

Before the apostles could exercise this power over souls, they would need to hear sins confessed aloud (or denounced publicly). Otherwise, they could not know what to bind or loose.

On Common Ground

Jesus was a Jew, a faithful son of Israel; so were His apostles. As Jews, they shared a common heritage, common memories, and a common language of religious experience. When Jesus spoke of forgiveness and confession, He drew upon those memories, that language, and that experience, knowing full well what His words would mean to the Jews who listened to Him.

When the apostles heard Jesus speak of forgiveness and confession, they understood Him in light of what they knew—the sacraments of the Old Covenant, which we considered in the last chapter. Again, Jesus didn't merely conclude the Old Covenant; He fulfilled it. He invested the trappings of the Old Covenant with greater capacities. In a mysterious way, the Old Covenant is concluded by—and included in—the New Covenant.

With that in mind, we should go back and reread what the apostles had to say on the subject, trying to understand their terms as they would have understood them—sharing with them the vocabulary and memory they shared with Jesus.

"If we confess our sins, [God] is faithful and just," said Saint John, "and will forgive our sins and cleanse us from all unrighteousness" (1 Jn 1:9). Saint Paul makes the further clarification that confession is something you do "with your mouth," not just with your heart and mind (Rom 10:10).

To whom, then, must we confess? To God, of course, but in the way that He ordained through Jesus Christ—to a priest. Saint James takes up the matter of confession at the end of his discussion of the sacramental duties of the clergy. The term he uses for clergymen is the Greek *presbuterous,* which literally means "elders," but which is the root of the English word *priest*:

Is any among you sick? Let him call for the elders [*pres-buterous*] of the church, and let them pray over him, anointing him with oil in the name of the Lord; and the prayer of faith will save the sick man, and the Lord will raise him up; and if he has committed sins, he will be forgiven. *Therefore* confess your sins to one another, and pray for one another, that you may be healed. (Jas 5:14–16)

Whenever you see the word *therefore* in Scripture, you have to ask yourself what it's there for. In this passage, James is clearly setting the practice of confession in connection with the priest's healing ministry. Because priests are healers, we call upon them to anoint our bodies when we are ill; and, *therefore*, even more eagerly, we go to them for the healing sacrament of forgiveness when our souls are sick with sin.

Note that Saint James does not exhort his congregation to confess their sins to Jesus alone; nor does he tell them to confess their sins silently, in their hearts. They may do all these things, and all to their credit, but they will not yet be faithful to the word of God preached by Saint James—not until they confess their sins aloud to "another," and specifically to a *presbyter*, a priest. The father figure is always in view.

Since the time of Adam, God had been guiding His people to make their confessions in a certain and efficacious way. Now, in the fullness of time, in the age of the Church of Jesus Christ, they could.

First Confessions

It can be helpful for us, at this point, to correct a common misunderstanding about the Church's first generations. Many people today mistakenly believe that Christianity represented an abrupt abandonment of the thought and the practices of ancient Israel—something so completely new that Jesus' contemporaries could hardly recognize it.

The truth, however, is quite the opposite. In fact, the first Christians held fast to many of the practices of early Judaism, which were now invested with a new power. Christians built their own synagogues and, until A.D. 70, they met at the Jerusalem Temple as well. Some observed the traditional Sabbath rest on Saturday as well as the Lord's Day on Sunday. Christians worshiped using many of the prayers, blessings, and liturgical forms of Judaism. In recent years, scholars have acquired a renewed appreciation for "the Jewish roots of Christian liturgy," and many great scholars have labored to demonstrate precisely how the ritual meals and sacrifices of Israel developed into the ritual meal and sacrifice that is at the heart of Christian life: the Mass.

The same is true for what the Church today calls the sacrament of confession, the sacrament of penance, the sacrament of forgiveness, the sacrament of reconciliation. The renewed Israel, the Catholic Church, did not abandon the powerful practice of their ancestors. Thus, we find Christians making confession in the first generation and every generation afterward.

The idea of confession appears twice in the oldest Jewish-Christian document we possess, apart from the Bible. The *Didache*, or *Teaching of the Apostles*, is a compilation of moral, doctrinal, and liturgical instructions. Some modern scholars say that parts of it were composed in Palestine or Antioch around A.D. 48.

"Thou shalt confess thy transgressions in the Church," commands the *Didache*, "and shalt not come unto prayer with an evil conscience" (4.14, Hoole translation). This comes at the end of a long list of moral commandments and instructions for penance.

A later chapter speaks of the importance of confession before receiving the Eucharist: "On the Lord's Day gather together, break bread, and give thanks [in Greek, *eucaristesate*], first confessing your sins so that your sacrifice may be pure" (14.1).

Later in the first century, probably between A.D. 70 and 80, we find the *Letter of Barnabas* repeating, verbatim, the command of the *Didache*: "Thou shalt confess thy transgressions in the Church, and shalt not come unto prayer with an evil conscience" (19).

Both the *Didache* and *Barnabas* may imply that Christians confessed their sins publicly; for "in the Church" can also be translated as "in the assembly." We know that, in many places, the Church did administer penance this way. The practice was abandoned in later centuries for pastoral reasons that are easy to guess—to spare the penitent the embarrassment, to spare the victims any shame, and for the sake of delicacy. This is one way the Church applied its mercy in an ever more merciful way.

We find our next witness at the turn of the next century, around A.D. 107: Saint Ignatius, bishop of Antioch, develops the idea of penance at the service of communion, as he writes to the people of Philadelphia, in Asia Minor. "To all those who repent, the Lord grants forgiveness, if they turn in penitence to the unity of God and to communion with the bishop" (*Letter to the Philadelphians* 8.1). The mark of the Christian who perseveres, according to Saint Ignatius, is faithfulness to confession. "For as many as are of God and of Jesus Christ are also with the bishop. And as many as shall, in the exercise of penance, return into the unity of the Church, these, too, shall belong to God, that they may live according to Jesus Christ" (*Letter to the Philadelphians* 3.2).

The alternative to confession was clear and chilling to the fathers of the Church. Said Pope Saint Clement of Rome in A.D. 96: "It is better for a man to confess his sins than to harden his heart" (*Letter to the Corinthians* 51.3).

Lapse-Sided Development

Though the sacrament has been with us from the day of Jesus' resurrection, Christians have practiced it in varying ways. The Church's doctrine of penance has developed, too, over time. In essence, the sacrament remains the same, though in particulars it might look different from age to age.

For example: In some places, early on, the bishops taught that certain sins—namely murder, adultery, and apostasy—could be confessed, but not absolved in this life. The Christian who committed these sins could never again receive communion, though he could hope for God's mercy in the hour of death. In other places, the bishops absolved such sins, but only after the sinners performed heavy penances, which might take years of difficult daily labor to complete. Over time, the Church modified these practices to make them less burdensome, to encourage Christians to find strength in the Eucharist for overcoming sin, and to keep sorry sinners from falling into despair.

Not all Christians were eager to welcome sinners back to the fold. Some argued that the Church was better off without such weaklings and misfits. The issue came to a head in North Africa when a man named Cyprian was bishop of Carthage (A.D. 248–258). It was a time of persecution; some Christians bravely went to their deaths, while others, sad to say, renounced Christ when faced with the threat of death or torture. Some of those who "lapsed" in the faith later regretted their decision and sought readmission to the Church. They met bitter opposition, however, from other Christians who had survived torture without renouncing Christ.

Cyprian insisted that repentant sinners should be readmitted to the Eucharist, after performing the penances prescribed by the Church. He begged all sinners, great and small, to take advantage of the sacrament of confession; for, in times of persecution, they knew neither the day nor the hour when they might be called. (Indeed, at all times, we know neither the day nor the hour when we will face our final judgment.) Said Saint Cyprian:

> I entreat you, beloved brethen, that each one should confess his own sin, while he who has sinned is still in this world, while his confession may be received, while the satisfaction and remission made by the priests are pleasing to the Lord. Let us turn to the Lord with our whole heart,

and, expressing our repentance for our sin with true grief, let us entreat God's mercy. . . . He Himself tells us in what manner we ought to ask: "Return to me," He says, "with all your heart, with fasting, with weeping, and with mourning; and rend your hearts, and not your garments." (Jl 2:12)

Cyprian could evoke the prophet Joel to exhort a "gentile" people to make their confession. Why? Because the prophet, the Savior, and the saint shared a single understanding of confession, conversion, and covenant. The Church's mission, from Christ Himself, was to proclaim that understanding as Gospel, as good news: "that repentance and forgiveness of sins should be preached in [Christ's] name to all nations, beginning from Jerusalem" (Lk 24:47).

In reading the fathers of the Church, we find that, wherever people professed Christ, they confessed their sins to the priests of the Church. We see this in the writings of Saint Irenaeus of Lyons, who served in France from A.D. 177 to 200. We find it in Tertullian, in North Africa, around A.D. 203; and Saint Hippolytus of Rome, around A.D. 215. The Egyptian scholar Origen, around A.D. 250, wrote of the "remission of sins through penance . . . when the sinner . . . is not ashamed to make known his sin to the priest of the Lord and to seek a cure according to the one who says, 'I acknowledged my sin to You, and I did not hide my iniquity; I said, "I will confess my transgressions to the Lord"; then You forgave the guilt of my sin' " (Ps 32:5).

The Best Seat in the House

It all comes together. God wishes our confession because it is a precondition of His mercy. This is His constant message, from the days of Adam and Cain through every generation of the Church of Jesus Christ. He was merciful from the beginning, but that mercy was revealed only gradually over time. Thus, in the Old Testament, He commanded the Israelites to build a "mercy seat"—the throne of God Himself—and place it in the Holy of Holies, over the Ark of the Covenant. There, the seat was inaccessible to everyone except the high priest, and even he could only approach once a year, on the Day of Atonement, when he would sprinkle the blood of a sacrifice for the sins of the people.

In the Old Covenant, the mercy seat was inaccessible, and it was empty. In the New Covenant, the seat is occupied at last, and by a high priest, Jesus, Who is able to sympathize with those who are weak (see Heb 4:15). Moreover, this high priest wants us not to stay away in fear and trembling, but to come forward. "Let us then with confidence draw near to the throne of grace, that we may receive mercy and find grace to help in time of need" (Heb 4:16).

This summons could only come with the fullness of the revelation of God. For mercy is God's greatest attribute. Why is it the greatest? Not because it makes us feel better, or because it's much more attractive to us than His power, wisdom, and goodness. It is His greatest attribute because it is the sum and substance of His power, His wisdom, and His goodness. We can distinguish those attributes that pertain to His might,

His knowledge, and His goodness. But mercy is something more. Indeed, it is the convergence of all three of those attributes. Mercy is God's power, wisdom, and goodness manifest in unity. God showed Moses that mercy was bound up with His very name, which to the Israelites meant His personal identity: "I will make all My goodness pass before you, and will proclaim before you My name 'The Lord'; and I will be gracious to whom I will be gracious, and show mercy on whom I will show mercy" (Ex 33:19).

Mercy has been fully revealed to us in Jesus Christ. It's important, however, that we understand it rightly. Mercy is not pity. Nor is it our free pass to "sin boldly" because we know we can get away with it in the end. As we'll see in a later chapter, mercy does not do away with all punishments, but rather ensures that each punishment will serve as a means of merciful remedy. Saint Thomas Aquinas insisted that mercy and justice are inseparable: "Justice and mercy are so united that they mutually temper each other: justice without mercy is cruelty, mercy without justice is disintegration."

The Catholic Encyclopedia puts it succinctly: "Mercy does not override justice, but rather transcends it and converts the sinner into a just person by bringing about repentance and openness to the Holy Spirit."

CHAPTER 4

TRUE CONFESSIONS:
SEALED WITH A SACRAMENT

LIKE ALL THE rites of the Church, confession has changed its look and feel down through the centuries—adapting to the different needs, and different moral climates, of different cultures. But confession has always remained the same in essence. It has remained what Christ intended it to be: the continuation, through all time, of His ministry of forgiveness and healing.

The rite has varied in many ways. In some times and in some places, Christians confessed their sins publicly before the congregation; in times like our own, confession is a private matter between the penitent and a priest. In the early Church, some bishops permitted a baptized believer to confess no more than once in the course of a lifetime. In times like our own, the Church recommends that we go at least once every month and requires that we go at least once a year.

Another element that has varied is the severity of the penances imposed by the Church. In the early days, those who confessed serious sins—such as murder, adultery, or apostasy—were readmitted to communion only after a long time spent in the Order of Penitents. These sinners might spend years in rigorous prayer, performing works of penance and almsgiving before they could again receive the Eucharist. Indeed, they were not even permitted to stay in the church building for the entire Mass; they were dismissed, along with any unbaptized people, before the beginning of the Eucharistic Prayer.

The monks of the Eastern deserts usually get credit for developing the practice of frequent, private confession. In the West, these practices found zealous promoters in Irish monks who traveled as missionaries throughout Europe. By the seventh century, the sacrament had, for the most part, assumed the appearance by which we know it today.

Even now, however, the sacrament can shift its shape. The Church permits more flexibility for this rite than for almost any other. The ordinary and "proper place to hear sacramental confessions is a church or an oratory," in a confessional booth with a "fixed grille," or screen. Sometimes, the penitent prefers the anonymity of confessing behind a screen to a priest who cannot see his face; at other times, he may prefer to make his confession face-to-face, as between old friends. Sometimes, men make their confession on a battlefield amid mortar fire; at other times, the spiritual healing comes at a hospital bed during a long last illness. I can testify to the varieties of confessional experience. At moments when no confessional was available, I've received the sacrament in many different ways: while walking along city streets, while riding in a car, and while waiting at an airport gate.

Yet the more things change, the more the sacrament remains the same. In this chapter, we'll look first at that essential core of the Church's teaching and then at the doctrine in action, as the Church celebrates the sacrament today.

The Magnificent Seven

Before we begin discussing the sacrament of confession, however, we should discuss sacraments in general.

What is a sacrament? In chapter 2, we used a classic definition: A sacrament is an outward sign of an inward reality. We can say further, as in another classic definition, that a sacrament of the New Covenant is "an outward sign instituted by Christ to give grace." Grace is God's life, which He shares with us through these actions that Christ has entrusted to His Church. The Church discerns seven such sacraments: baptism, Eucharist, confirmation, confession, anointing of the sick, marriage, and Holy Orders. These seven are traditionally divided into sacraments of initiation (baptism, Eucharist, confirmation), sacraments of healing (confession and anointing of the sick), and sacraments of vocation (marriage and Holy Orders).

The sacraments of the New Covenant are certainly "new" with Jesus Christ, but not in the sense that they are novelties. For the New Covenant itself is not new in that sense. It is, rather, a renewal of what the early Christians called the "eternal covenant," the covenant that transcends time. We might more accurately translate it as the "Renewed Covenant"—the consummate renewal of what God had done again and again in history.

He made a covenant. In the ancient world, a covenant was the legal and liturgical means by which two parties created a family bond. Marriage was a covenant; the adoption of a child was a covenant. Whenever God made a covenant with man—as He did with Adam, Noah, Abraham, Moses, and David—He renewed a family bond between Himself and His people. The covenant was usually ratified by certain outward signs: an oath, a common meal, and a sacrifice.

All of God's work in the Old Covenant did not vanish into irrelevance with the coming of Jesus Christ. There is no yawning chasm separating the Old Covenant from the New. The New is promised in the Old; and the Old is fulfilled in the New. Thus, the Old Covenant signs—the oath, the meal, the sacrifice—find perfection in the New Covenant sacraments. "Behold," said Jesus, "I make all things new" (Rev 21:5). He renews all things when He establishes His perfectly renewed covenant.

All the sacraments of the New Covenant are ordered toward the Eucharist, which is both a family meal and a sacrifice. All the sacraments invoke the sacred name of God, and so all have binding power as oaths. Moreover, in the New Covenant, as in the Old, "the liturgy of the renewal of the covenant" has "a particular link with the remission of sins." It is in the New Covenant, however, that that power is made perfect and the forgiveness complete.

(The Latin word for *oath,* incidentally, is *sacramentum,*

from which we get the English word *sacrament*. The Church's usage of *sacramentum,* meaning simultaneously "a sworn oath" and "a sacred rite," is recorded as early as A.D. 110.)

Confession prepares us to receive the Eucharist more worthily. It makes us a purer vessel to hold the divine life given us in the grace of the sacraments. Confession gives us the right dispositions for our renewal of the covenant, our family bond with almighty God. Without this forgiveness, we might approach Him as slaves approach their master, with our eyes cast down to the ground. But with the words of absolution, we are empowered to look upward with the eyes of innocence, as children look up to a loving father.

Tradition's Conditions

How does Confession do this? The details of the rite have sometimes changed; but, says the *Catechism of the Catholic Church* (*CCC*), "Beneath the changes in discipline and celebration . . . , the same *fundamental structure* is to be discerned" (n. 1448). The sacrament of penance is made up of two equally essential elements. On the one hand, there's our work, the work of the repentant sinner; and, on the other hand, there's the work God does through the Church.

It's all God's work, in a sense, because even the works we do are the actions of a sinner "who undergoes conversion *through the action of the Holy Spirit*" (*CCC*, n. 1448, italics added). We, however, must give consent and struggle to fulfill God's will. What actions, then, make up our part of the sacrament? Tradition names three: contrition, confession, and satisfaction. In other words, the sacrament demands (1) that we should be sorry for our sins, (2) that we should state our sorrow clearly by naming our sins, and (3) that we should complete the work of penance or restitution assigned to us by our priest-confessor. Let's look at these one by one.

1. We must be sorry for our sins. The technical word for this sorrow is *contrition*. Without such sorrow, we cannot receive this sacrament; for the essence of the sacrament, on our part, is our apology to God, Whom we have offended. Our contrition need not be perfect; it need not spring from a motive of pure love. We might, for example, be motivated by fear of God's punishment. That's a good start, and God's grace will complete the work in us and make up for what is lacking in our sorrow. We must, however, offer some resolution to change our lives and to avoid, in the future, the sins we have confessed from our past. We should even resolve to avoid the company and the places that might tempt us to sin. Tradition calls this resolution a "firm purpose of amendment," and it is formulated well in many of the prayers we call Acts of Contrition: "I firmly resolve, with the help of Your grace, to sin no more and to avoid the near occasions of sin."

Some people think, "Well, as long as Catholics tell their sins to the priests, they can go on committing sins, whenever they want." And this is not just a Catholic issue; it's true of any religion that emphasizes repentance. The repentance has to be genuine, and so does the firm purpose of amendment. Harvard philosopher William James once said, "I would sin like David, if only I could repent like David" (see Ps 51).

That, however, is a total delusion. The truth is, unless the sinner is truly sorry—unless that sinner approaches the sacrament with contrition and confesses all known serious sins sincerely, humbly, and completely—the sacrament does not confer the absolution—the sins are not forgiven. What's more, the sinner has committed the added sin of sacrilege.

Jesus Himself insisted upon a change of life when He pronounced absolution. He faced the woman caught in adultery and told her He would not condemn her. But then He added, "Go, and do not sin again" (Jn 8:11). Today, through His Church, He asks no less.

2. We must confess our sins. Scripture makes a distinction between two types of sin: mortal sin and venial sin (see 1 Jn 5:16–17). Mortal sin is, as its name implies, the more deadly of the two, for it chokes off God's life in the soul. Mortal sin kills us spiritually. Mortal sin always involves "grave matter"—the most important things in life. Even nonbelievers will often recognize the gravity of these offenses. Thus, for example, murder is a mortal sin, and it is universally recognized as a crime; the same goes for grand theft, perjury, and adultery. Other grave matter, however, can be seen only with the eyes of faith. Thus, for example, it is a mortal sin to miss Mass on a Sunday.

Every time we go to the sacrament of penance, we must confess any and all mortal sins committed since our last confession. We must clearly state the types of mortal sin we've committed and the number of times we've committed them. If we hold back any mortal sins, then we have not made a valid confession. Indeed, to deliberately withhold confessing a mortal sin is itself a mortal sin. Since a sacrament is an oath before God, such nondisclosure represents a sort of perjury.

We are not strictly required to confess our venial sins—the *Catechism* calls them "everyday faults"—but the Church, the saints, and the mystics have always recommended this (see *CCC*, n. 1458).

It's important to remember, in our confession, that we're not telling God anything He doesn't already know. He knows our sins better than we do. He knew Adam's sin when He invited Adam to confess. He knew Cain's when He invited Cain to confess. He wants us to confess not for His good, but for ours, because He knows that confession is a necessary step in our process of healing toward holiness.

Confession is necessary, but there are some very limited circumstances in which a priest may dispense with confession and grant absolution anyway. In times of dire emergency, when a number of people are in immediate danger of death—in the heat of battle, or if a plane is about to crash—a priest may pronounce a "general absolution." Even this requires that penitents must be sorry for their sins, though it dispenses with their need to confess their sins. Even then, the penitent, if he should survive, must go as soon as possible to make an ordinary sacramental confession.

3. We must complete the work of penance or restitution. After receiving absolution from the priest, we perform some act of penance assigned by our priest-confessor. It might be a prayer, a work of mercy, an act of almsgiving, or an act of self-denial, such as fasting (see *CCC*, n. 1460). These are usually measured out to correspond to the gravity and nature of our sins.

It's important that we do this promptly, so that we don't forget. If we do forget, the absolution is still valid; but we have missed a tremendous opportunity to grow spiritually, and we have perhaps committed a venial sin as well.

Since our sins are offenses against almighty God, our small works of penance could never make full restitution, for our offenses are graver when committed against persons of greater dignity. In the context of an analogy from civil society: It's one thing for you to try to punch your next-door neighbor; it's quite another if you try to punch the president of the country. For the former offense, you might be slapped with a suit or a complaint; but for the latter, you would certainly serve time, and you might even be shot. No one has greater dignity than God; His dignity is infinite; and so we could never truly make up for our offenses to Him.

But Christ can make up for what we lack, and He does so in the sacrament. Indeed, that is the reason for the sacrament. The work of reconciliation is not primarily ours. It is Christ's, and it was accomplished on the cross. Through the sacraments, we come to share in His work, by His grace, and to know His benefits.

We do penance, then, to provide restitution and repair the damages done by sin, but also to restore and strengthen our bond of love with Christ and the people of God. In this context, I can't help but quote the *Catechism* again: "Such penances help configure us to Christ, who alone expiated our sins once for all. They allow us to become coheirs with the risen Christ, 'provided we suffer with him' [Rom 8:17]" (*CCC*, n. 1460).

The Other Side of the Screen

All of this implies that there is someone on the receiving end of our confession. There is, of course, and He is Jesus Christ. Indeed, only God can forgive sins. But Jesus has delegated His power to forgive to His Church, personified by His priests. He breathed the Holy Spirit upon those first clergymen, the apostles, and He said, "Receive the Holy Spirit. If you forgive the sins of any, they are forgiven." And, in doing so, the Gospel here uses the same Greek verb used elsewhere to describe Jesus' unique power to forgive (see Lk 7:48; Mt 9:2). In a sense, nothing had changed. The power of forgiveness still rested with God alone. Only now, God was empowering others to forgive *in His name*, as a sure and sacramental sign.

Through the priest, Christ forgives sinners and finds some way the sinner can make it up to God. The priest assigns the penance. The Church also prays for the sinner and does penance with him. In addition, the priest may give the penitent some advice on overcoming sin and growing in virtue.

The most important thing the priest does, however, is to pronounce the words of absolution. If we have done our part—contrition, confession, and satisfaction—then these words work a tremendous, divine power in us. For the formula of absolution is not God's promise to look the other

way, or ignore our sins, or put the past behind Him. Such no-
tions are absurd and indeed incompatible with a God Who is
omniscient and eternal.

The words of absolution are not the mere babbling of a
clergyman. They are the word of God, which He pronounces with power over us—just as He pronounced with
power over the waters at the dawn of creation—just as He
pronounced with power over the bread which He declared
to be His body. God's word is creative and efficacious. That's
the kind of power He wields in the sacrament of confession
as well. To create is to fashion something out of nothing.
With the words of absolution, God renews us as if we were
a new creation. When King David prayed: "Create in me a
clean heart, O God!" (Ps 51:10), he meant it. God, for His
part, has promised that He will answer such prayers: "A new
heart I will give you . . . I will take out of your flesh the
heart of stone and give you a heart of flesh" (Ezek 36:26).

This power is most manifest after a penitent confesses a
mortal sin. For such a sinner is surely more dead than Lazarus
was after four days in the tomb (see Jn 11:38–44). And mortal sins are more offensive and shameful than the stench of
any dead man's corpse. The lingering effects of such sins bind
us hand and foot, like the bandages wound about the corpse
of Lazarus, and they keep us from doing good, experiencing
love, or achieving lasting peace.

Yet all that changes with the words of absolution. When
penitent sinners hear those words, they should experience no
less a shock than that long-ago dead man did when he heard
Jesus say, "Lazarus, come out!" Sin is a greater death than

cessation of bodily life; so, through absolution, Christ works a greater miracle than He worked at the tomb of Lazarus.

Indeed, Tradition calls this miracle "the grace of resurrection." Why? Because, as one theologian has written, "it results in the raising of the spiritually dead to the life of grace." It is also called the grace "of healing, because by it, with the sinner's willing cooperation, the wounds of sin are cicatrized and cured."

The formula of absolution expresses all the essential elements of the sacrament of confession.

God, the Father of mercies,
through the death and the resurrection of His Son
has reconciled the world to Himself
and sent the Holy Spirit among us
for the forgiveness of sins;
through the ministry of the Church
may God give you pardon and peace,
and I absolve you from your sins
in the name of the Father, and of the Son, and of the Holy
Spirit.

Who Needs a Priest?

Non-Catholics often object that the priest is unnecessary in this process, that Christians can confess their sins directly to God. No doubt we can; but we cannot be assured of forgiveness unless we go about our confession in the way that God Himself intended. We have already discussed the passage in John where Jesus commissioned His clergy to forgive sins. We have already discussed James's exhortation to confession, which comes at the conclusion of his discussion of the clergy and the sacraments. The New Testament foundation for the sacrament is solid, and it has been cited in support of the practice ever since the very first generations of Christianity.

God's sovereignty is not threatened when He shares His power with others. Indeed, the power remains His own. Christ is still the Priest behind the priest. He is the Priest within the priest, and he is the Priest acting through the priest. So we don't go to the priest instead of going to Christ. We don't go to the confessional instead of going to the Lord of Mercy. We go to the Lord of Mercy, and He tells us to go to the confessional. Christ has instituted these creaturely means for the health of our soul. Sin is like an infection for which we need to go to the doctor to obtain the right prescription, for the right dosage; and then we follow the advice because we trust the authority.

This is something that the early Church saw clearly. In the fourth century, Saint Basil said: "Confession of sins must be made to those to whom the dispensing of God's sacraments has been committed." In the same century, Saint Ambrose declared that "Christ granted this power to the apostles, and from the apostles it has been transmitted to the office of the priests alone." And how awesome is that power! Saint John Chrysostom, in the fifth century, wrote that "Priests have received a power which God has not given either to angels or to archangels: . . . they are able to forgive our sins."

God alone possesses supernatural power to work miracles, but He does appoint miracle workers when He calls certain ministers, like Moses, who do things that no human could do. God uses creaturely means because that's how He is glorified, by raising us up, as a good father raises his children. So if we see priests doing things that God alone can do, that isn't proof that the priest is detracting from God. It's proof that God is fathering us, just as He promised.

What's more, He's doing it just as He always has: through a covenant, a sworn oath, a family bond, a blessing. And so we begin every confession: *Bless me, Father.*

CHAPTER 5

What's Wrong
with the World:
A Sinthesis

W HAT'S WRONG WITH the world?" is a question that leads nicely into long, ponderous sermons or thick volumes on the decline of civilization. G. K. Chesterton answered it with two short words: "I am."

It's the essence of confession that we all do the same. To confess our sins is to accept responsibility for our actions and their consequences, to take the blame squarely on our own shoulders, to admit that the decision to sin was ours alone, and to do all this—as best we can—without excuses, disclaimers, or euphemisms.

This does not come easily to us. Though we will occasionally admit some tangential relationship with minor wrongdoing, we usually follow up quickly with "but . . ." and then describe the exonerating circumstance. "I was only doing what so-and-so did." "I was only following orders." "How was I to know . . . ?" "It's the way I was brought up." Or even the famous blame-throwing of comedian Flip Wilson: "The devil made me do it."

What's wrong with the world? It's easy to probe the ills of the nation, the Church, and the planet and come up with a grave diagnosis: It's the collapse of family values, the destruction of the ecosystem, or the latest moral crisis in the Church. But it takes all the strength we can muster to stand up at Mass and honestly say, "I have sinned through my own fault, in my thoughts and in my words, in what I have done and in what I have failed to do."

Sin-Cerity

It takes more courage still to kneel down in the confessional and accuse ourselves of each sin by name. Yet this has always been the inevitable corollary to a close relationship with God. We all want to know God's nearness, His help, His fatherly love. However, all that comes, inevitably, with an increased awareness of His goodness, His purity, and His perfect judgment. The prophet Isaiah suddenly found himself in the presence of God, surrounded by glory, attended by angels. What did he do? He made his confession: "Woe is me! For I am lost; for I am a man of unclean lips, and I dwell in the midst of a people of unclean lips; for my eyes have seen the King, the Lord of hosts!" (Is 6:5). The apostle Peter witnessed a single small miracle and immediately threw himself at the feet of Jesus, begging, "Depart from me, for I am a sinful man, O Lord" (Lk 5:8).

Sin is not out there; it's deep inside you and me. "For out of the heart come evil thoughts, murder, adultery, fornication, theft, false witness, slander. These are what defile a man" (Mt 15:19–20).

What's wrong with the world? *I* am, because *I* sin, and my sins well up from the darkness in my own heart.

It's a simple matter, really, as simple as two words, a grand total of three letters. Sin itself, however, is a complicated matter, which requires us to make many distinctions. There are many kinds of sin. "Sins can be distinguished according to their objects . . . or according to the virtues they oppose, by excess or by defect; or according to the commandments they violate. They can also be classed according to whether they concern God, neighbor, or oneself; they can be divided into spiritual and carnal sins, or again as sins in thought, word, deed, or omission" (*CCC*, n. 1853). There are almost too many ways to slice this foul-tasting pie.

In this chapter, we'll try to make a basic catalog of the kinds of sin. It's an unpleasant business, but somebody's got to do it, and that somebody is you and me.

Graceful Habits

It's impossible to understand sin unless we first understand grace. We can't understand what we lose unless we first understand what we have. For grace is what we lose when we sin; and there's no greater loss we can suffer.

With baptism, we are made "partakers of the divine nature" (2 Pet 1:4). We are incorporated into Christ, Who is the only begotten Son of God, and so we share His sonship. We share in His Trinitarian life. The essential effect of baptism, then, is our adoption into the family of God. As an adopted son or daughter, the Christian can call God "Father," in union with the only Son.

This divine life, which we receive, is called sanctifying grace. The English word *grace* comes from the Greek word *charis*, meaning "gift." *Sanctifying* comes from the Latin words for "making holy." God alone is holy; but, through a free gift, He enables us to share His holiness. There is no greater gift we can receive. (See *CCC*, n. 1997.)

Tradition tells us that this gift is "habitual"—that is, it's a steady state, "a stable and supernatural disposition that enables the soul to live with God, to act by His love" (*CCC*, supplementary glossary). To live this life is to live in the state of grace.

We, however, are free to accept the gift or to reject it by sin. Sin is any action—any thought, word, deed, or omission—that offends God, violates His law, or dishonors the order of His creation.

The Great Omission

Note that we can even sin by omission—by inaction, by silence, by *not* doing something we should rightly have done. Sometimes these sins result from neglect and sometimes from choice; either way, it is sin. The Letter to the Hebrews tells us: "If the message declared by angels was valid and every transgression or disobedience received a just retribution, how shall we escape if we *neglect* such a great salvation?" (2:2–3). Indeed, when Jesus speaks of judgment and hellfire in Matthew 25, He speaks almost exclusively in terms of sins of omission and neglect. "Lord, when did we see You hungry or thirsty or a stranger or naked or sick or in prison, and did not minister to You?" (v. 44). Jesus' answer allows for no omission: "Truly, I say to you, as you did it not to one of the least of these, you did it not to Me" (v. 45).

Neglect is hardly a negligible sin. In fact, it can be mortal. It is no excuse, for example, to say that we missed Mass on Sunday because we forgot that it was Sunday. The "message declared by angels" commands us that we must *remember* the Lord's Day and keep it holy. Forgetting is a direct violation of the command to remember. Thus, in our moral life, as in our workaday life, negligence can kill.

Just as we can damage our natural life by mutilation, or end our human life by suicide, so we can damage or end our supernatural life by sin. And just as we receive this life of grace through a sacrament, so we must have it restored through a sacrament—the sacrament of confession.

Mortality Rates

This brings us to the first distinction between types of sin, a division we touched upon briefly in the last chapter. There is venial sin, and there is mortal sin. Put simply, venial sins damage our supernatural life; mortal sins end our supernatural life. Venial sins mark spiritual illness; mortal sin means spiritual death.

Mortal sin destroys life more certainly than any weapon

or disease. A man who has committed mortal sin is more dead than a week-old corpse—even though his mind and body continue to show every sign of biological life.

This death is the only thing that Jesus advised His followers to fear: "Do not fear those who kill the body but cannot kill the soul; rather fear him who can destroy both soul and body in hell" (Mt 10:28). Hell—the "lake of fire" in the Book of Revelation—is the ultimate consequence when someone chooses to commit a mortal sin. For if divine life is choked off in a person, that person cannot share God's life in heaven. If we have no communion with Christ, we are incapable of life in the Trinity.

What makes a sin mortal rather than venial? There are three necessary conditions: grave matter, full knowledge, and deliberate consent.

The Church's tradition and the Scriptures make clear what sorts of sins are mortal. Sometimes, an individual's guilt may be reduced because he was unaware that a certain action was sinful—perhaps he was misinformed—or because he did not have full possession of his will—perhaps he was forced or manipulated. We must, however, avoid the temptation to apply these conditions too lavishly, since we bear a certain responsibility for our own ignorance of Christian morality or for the particular circumstances that prove, for us, an occasion of sin.

In order for our sacramental confession to be valid, we must confess all mortal sins (at least those we're aware of) that have been committed since our last confession.

Hardened, Not Pardoned

Is there a sin so deadly that it can never be forgiven? Jesus said there is: "every sin and blasphemy; but whoever speaks against the Holy Spirit will not be forgiven. And whoever says a word against the Son of Man will be forgiven; but whoever speaks against the Holy Spirit will not be forgiven, either in this age or in the age to come" (Mt 12:31–32).

Theologians, saints, and sinners have debated the meaning of this passage for the better part of two millennia. Some favor so broad a definition that the majority of people might despair of ever reaching heaven. Others strain the broth so thin that unforgivable sin seems almost uncommittable.

The Church teaching, as always, strikes the perfect balance. First, the Church warns us that we can indeed place ourselves beyond forgiveness. In the words of the *Catechism*: "There are no limits to the mercy of God, but anyone who deliberately refuses to accept His mercy by repenting, rejects the forgiveness of his sins and the salvation offered by the Holy Spirit. Such hardness of heart can lead to final impenitence and eternal loss" (*CCC*, n. 1864).

This seems to be common sense. If we cut off our own arms and legs, we should despair of ever winning the Olympic decathlon. If we cut off our own repentance, we should certainly not expect to obtain forgiveness.

The pharisees, of whom Jesus spoke in the "unforgivable" passage, did not simply refuse to repent of their errors, but they went on to accuse the Son of God of the most heinous sins. Not only did they refuse to recognize His power as divine; they accused Him of acting by "power of the prince of demons" (Mt 12:24). Thus, they inflicted upon themselves a spiritual blindness that was permanent and final. Their example should inspire a holy fear in all of us. Yet we must never despair.

Is such sin rare or common? Pope John Paul II said: "It is certainly to be hoped that very few persist to the end in this attitude of rebellion or even defiance of God." He goes on to quote Saint Thomas Aquinas: "Considering the omnipotence and mercy of God, no one should despair of the salvation of anyone in this life."

No Small Matter

"All wrongdoing is sin," says Saint John, "but there is sin which is not mortal" (1 Jn 5:17). Venial sin is the name we give to faults of lesser gravity. There's no such thing as a sinless lie; but not all lies weigh as heavily as perjury under oath or false accusation. Thus, perjury is a mortal sin; but lying about your age, for vanity's sake, might be venial.

Venial sin weakens our will. It wounds us in the spirit, though it does not kill us. Pope John Paul II wrote: "Venial sin does not deprive the sinner of sanctifying grace, friendship with God, charity, and consequently eternal happiness." We can get to heaven if we die with venial sins unconfessed, but they must first be cleansed from our soul; for "nothing unclean shall enter" God's eternal life (Rev 21:27).

We are not obligated to confess our venial sins. Indeed, they can be forgiven in other ways. For example, every time we receive Holy Communion, our venial sins are wiped away entirely. We can ask and obtain forgiveness for venial sins by reciting a simple, sincere Act of Contrition. The Bible tells us that venial sins can even be forgiven through the intercession of others: "If anyone sees his brother committing what is not a mortal sin, he will ask, and God will give him life for those whose sin is not mortal" (1 Jn 5:16).

Still, we do best if we discern these smaller sins and begin to conquer them now, by seeking forgiveness in the confessional. The sacrament will give us grace, then, to overcome them in the future; and the priest-confessor can give us very specific, practical advice on how best to correspond to that grace with action. The introduction to the rite of penance tells us that the confession of venial sins is not a mere "psychological exercise." It is, rather, "a constant and renewed commitment to refine the grace of baptism so that, while we carry about in our bodies the dying of Christ Jesus, His life may be ever more revealed in us." No sin—no matter how small—is compatible with the life of Christ, Who is forever sinless. If we want to grow in His life, if we want His life to grow in us, we must be firm in our resolve not to sin at all, or at least (for starters) to sin less frequently.

We need not be discouraged if we continue to fall into venial sin. But neither should we give up our resolve to put off such sins entirely. For we must not underestimate the damage venial sins can do. Again, some lies are less serious than others, but there's no such thing as a lie that's "little" or "white." Pope John Paul II taught: "It must not be forgotten that venial sins can inflict dangerous wounds on the sinner."

Venial sins, especially if they are habitual, make us ever weaker in our resistance to mortal sin. They are the thin edge of sin's wedge in our lives.

Confessing these sins, however, provides a powerful counteractive force. Said Pope John Paul II: "The confession of these sins with a view to sacramental forgiveness, in fact, singularly helps us grow aware of our condition as sinners before God in order to make amends." Thus armed with grace and good advice, we can continue resolutely on the path to our perfection. "In this way the penitent tends toward 'that perfect man who is Christ come to full stature' [Eph 4:13]; besides, 'professing the truth in love,' he is spurred on to 'grow to the full maturity of Christ the head' [Eph 4:15]."

No Sin Is an Island

All sin is personal. Someone, somewhere makes the decision to commit this or that particular sin, whether it's venial or mortal. But no sin is an island. Sins engender other sins, not only in the sinner but in others as well. When we sin, we change the moral climate, perhaps imperceptibly at first; but then our faults roll in with the small faults of many other people and cause a sort of moral snowball effect. One person's small sins give tacit permission for a bystander's slightly larger sins, and this process of peer degradation continues—until someone decides to reverse the downward momentum.

All sin has a social dimension. Moreover, we have a responsibility for the sins of others when we cooperate in them:

- by participating directly and voluntarily in them;
- by ordering, advising, praising, or approving them (even by smiling at them);
- by not disclosing or not hindering them when we have an obligation to do so;
- by protecting evildoers (see *CCC*, n. 1868).

We mustn't just stand there. When people are sinning, we're morally bound to do something. Saint Ambrose wrote: "Not only for every idle word, but for every idle silence shall we be called to account." Remember, the biblical model for minding one's own business is Cain, who asked, "Am I my brother's keeper?" The question itself betrays his disordered thinking. He was his brother's *brother*, and that should have been enough to justify his concern. If we are God's children, we must come to see others as our brothers and sisters; and so we must correct them when they need correction, and help them to grow. Moreover, we must count on our siblings in Christ to correct us when we're going astray. This is how life goes on in a fully functional family.

The sins we confess are personal sins and actual sins. Mine are mine. Yours are yours. We each take responsibility for them. Yet they are not the only sins that affect us and weaken us. Since we live in a society, since we live in families, we can't help but be influenced by the sins of others. Though every sin has just one parent—the individual sinner who chooses to sin—all sins can trace a common genealogy. All sins are, in a sense, descended from the original sin.

Dead Wrong

What was that sin? Let's look at the story of how it all began, in the book of beginnings, the Book of Genesis. God created the first man, Adam, in a state of grace. He was in a state of divine sonship by virtue of the grace conferred upon him when God "breathed into his nostrils the breath of life" (Gen 2:7). In addition to supernatural life, Adam possessed perfect natural powers and preternatural gifts: immortality, for example, and an intelligence endowed with superhuman powers. What's more, he lived in paradise alongside the perfect wife, with whom he shared dominion over all the earth.

God asked only one thing in return. "And the Lord God commanded the man, saying, 'You may freely eat of every tree of the garden; but of the tree of the knowledge of good and evil you shall not eat, for in the day that you eat of it you shall die' " (Gen 2:16–17). In hindsight, it seems like little to ask—all the riches of the world plus everlasting life, in exchange for abstinence from a certain sort of fruit! It seems almost too easy. But, for Adam and Eve, it was to become the most severe trial.

Before I go any further, I should point out an oddity in the Hebrew text of Genesis. The passage translated above as "you shall die" does not accurately represent the original. The Hebrew actually repeats the word *die*, so that it reads "you shall die die." Now, in Hebrew, repetition serves to intensify a word (to make it "more" or "surely"); but it seems odd for us to find a repetition of the word *die*. After all, you can't get any deader than dead.

What could this mean? The greatest of the ancient Jewish commentators, Philo of Alexandria, explained that there are two types of death: the death of the body and the death of the soul. "The death of the man is the separation of the soul from the body," he wrote. "But the death of the soul is the decay of virtue and the bringing in of wickedness. It is for this reason that God says not only 'die' but 'die the death,' indicating not the death common to us all, but that special death, which is that of the soul becoming entombed in passions and wickedness of all kinds. And this death is practically the antithesis of the death which awaits us all."

Yet that death is precisely what Adam chose.

Serpentine Slide

His choice seems either insane or stupid; but it was neither. Adam faced just a single adversary in the garden. In artwork, this "serpent" is usually portrayed as an unimposing garden snake, but that is not what the text of Genesis (3:1) suggests. The word in Hebrew is *nahash*, which has a fairly wide spectrum of meaning. It is used most often to denote a snake (see Num 21:6–9), but it is also used in reference to evil dragons (see Is 27:1; cf. Rev 12:3, 9). Across this spectrum of usage, the word *nahash* generally refers to something that bites (see Prv 23:32), with venom (see Ps 58:4).

What is clear is that Adam faced a formidable, life-threatening force. Moreover, the serpent seized on something that would have been natural to any creature with a physical body: the instinctive dread of dying. The serpent seduces Adam with promises, but he also presents an implied threat. The *Catechism of the Catholic Church* identifies the serpent as Satan (see n. 391) and spells out the power he had both to seduce Adam (n. 391) and to harm him physically and spiritually (nn. 395 and 394).

Adam feared the beast and feared death. Indeed, he feared for his life more than he feared for his wife; for he did not step forward to protect her. He feared death more than he feared offending God by sin. He would not step forward with a martyr's courage. He could not even bring himself to call out to God for help. In pride and in fear, he kept silent. Then, with his wife, he disobeyed the command of the Lord. They ate the forbidden fruit. And the rest is salvation history.

Did he and Eve die? If by death you mean the spiritual death discussed by Philo, then, yes, they did. If by death you mean mortal sin and the loss of divine grace, then, yes, they did die—more truly and more completely than if their bodies had been blown apart by a diabolical grenade.

They had died the death. Why would God subject Adam and Eve to such a trial? Because something greater lay on the other side of it. Adam and Eve were given the life of grace, but that was only penultimate. God had intended that grace to be a seed of glory. Adam was made *in* paradise, but made *for* heaven. God wanted Adam to share the inner life of the Trinity, which is complete self-giving: The Father pours

Himself out in love for the Son; the Son returns that love completely with the gift of His own life; and that love shared by the Father and the Son is itself a divine person, the Holy Spirit. In order for Adam to share that life, he would have to begin living it on earth, in paradise. He would have to offer himself completely in sacrifice. And that is what he failed to do.

Adam was unwilling to lay down his own life for the sake of his love of God, or to save the life of his beloved. That refusal to sacrifice was Adam's original sin.

Fault Lines

Original sin is the term we use to describe mankind's first transgression—Adam's fall. It is also the term we use to describe the consequences or effects of that fall. For Adam, original sin was a personal, actual sin. For us, it's an impersonal sin, not an actual sin. But here we distinguish; we do not separate, because it's all of a piece. There is a bond that unites sin in all its forms.

When teachers discuss the mystery of original sin, they often use the metaphor of a "stain on the soul." But that's only a metaphor. Sin isn't essentially a stain; it isn't a spiritual substance. It isn't a thing at all. It is, rather, the *lack* of something, the absence of something, namely sanctifying grace. The indwelling life of the Trinity was evacuated from human nature by Adam's sin. That's what original sin is. We have to get at it by explaining what it isn't. It's the absence of something necessary for human beings to reach their divinely appointed end. The absence of sanctifying grace certainly does plunge us into darkness and blindness and death.

But it's critically important for us to recognize that original sin is not *something* that's transmitted biologically or psychologically. Yet at the same time we can speak of original sin as being something hereditary. Pope Pius XI wrote that "Original sin is the hereditary but impersonal fault of Adam's descendants."

Even that word choice—*fault*—might lead you to believe that original sin is something that renders us guilty. But it isn't. Think of *fault* here in the sense of the San Andreas Fault, the fracture in the earth's crust that renders California vulnerable to devastating earthquakes. That's what the *fault* of original sin does in the soul. It isn't *my fault*, but it's like a fault line that runs through my soul and inclines me to be separated from God.

Original sin is the hereditary but impersonal fault of Adam's descendants: "[O]ne man's trespass led to condemnation for all men . . . [B]y one man's disobedience many were made sinners, who have sinned in him" (Rom 5:18–19).

The mystery, of course, is how we sinned in Adam. We sinned in Adam, in a sense, because there is a mystical solidarity we share with him, based upon two realities: *biologically*, we're his descendants; and *theologically*, he's our covenant head. As our father, he is our representative in making the covenant with God. Since he broke the covenant, we, his progeny, inherit the consequences. Consider an analogy from human relations: If I mismanaged my business affairs and ended by declaring bankruptcy before passing my estate to my sons and daughter, my creditors could pursue my children, now rendered debtors through our family bond.

In effect, original sin means the loss of sanctifying grace and, therefore, the loss of eternal life. Eternal life is not merely everlasting life. The soul is immortal, and people in hell will live everlastingly, though miserably. Eternal life is more than everlasting. It is God's life, divine life. God alone is eternal because He utterly transcends time. So when we speak of eternal life, we're talking about sharing in the very being and communion of the Father, Son, and Holy Spirit. And that's what humanity lost through original sin.

Original sin is hereditary but impersonal. It is contracted, not committed; and we contract original sin without consent. That is why God can remove original sin without personal consent, as He does with newborn babies on their baptism day.

The same thing cannot be said for actual sin. Actual sin can only be committed through informed consent. And so it can only be removed through informed consent. That's why we need confession.

The Law of (Moral) Gravity

It can be helpful to keep in mind that sin is like a terminal—but curable—illness, one that afflicts all of the organs of the body. Only in this case, it affects the eternal life of the soul.

Are people better off not knowing that they're sick? Or how accessible (though difficult) the cure is? Are they any happier not being told how serious—but also how treatable—their condition is?

For me, the key is remembering that sin is more than breaking laws, it is breaking lives—our own and others'. Likewise, our spiritual life is far more precious—and fragile—than physical life. And far more fulfilling, eternally speaking.

Just because people don't recognize all (or any) of God's laws, and how they reflect His loving concern for our spiritual and physical health, doesn't change the fact that it's all still true. If an overwhelming majority of Americans wanted to abolish the law of gravity, and so both houses of Congress voted to repeal it, and the president signed it into law—what would happen if the president and all the congressmen decided to celebrate their "liberation" by jumping off the White House roof? They wouldn't break the law of gravity, of course; their fall would demonstrate gravity, and that law would break them and whatever bones hit first.

What people often forget is that the moral laws of God are just as firmly fixed as the physical laws—it's just that the results of sin are not as visible or immediately painful as broken bones.

That's why the Church has to get the word out—both the bad news of sin's deadly effect, and the Good News of Christ as the only total cure. And again, that's why we need confession.

CHAPTER 6

SACRAMENTAL CONFECTION: WHAT'S SO SWEET ABOUT SINNING?

A S A UNIVERSITY professor, I sometimes assign students to read Saint Augustine's *Confessions*. The book has almost universal appeal. Even the most worldly and unconverted readers find themselves captivated by Augustine's brilliant style—or at least by his suggestive remembrances of a misspent youth. In some cases, the saint's book gets read primarily because his sins were scarlet. The careful self-analysis of Augustine's *Confessions* can be tremendously helpful to those of us who are preparing our own sacramental confessions.

There is one passage, however, that puzzles even devout readers. It's more than a passage, actually. Augustine spends *seven chapters* describing a brief moment he spent late one night when he was sixteen years old. What thrilling escapade could consume such a magnificent mind to that extent?

Augustine and his friends pilfered a few pears from his neighbor's orchard.

Readers find this baffling. Augustine gave long years of

his life to the pursuit of sins of the flesh. He had mistresses. He conceived a child out of wedlock. With no less ardor did he give himself over to sins of the spirit. He tracked exotic spiritualities far into the regions of heresy and apostasy. He skipped out of Christian instruction and gave his soul over to the care of a non-Christian guru. Many and great were his transgressions. Yet no single sin does he subject to such minute analysis as the petty theft of pears when he was sixteen.

Again and again, Augustine asks why he committed the sin. It wasn't that he was hungry; in fact, he wasn't. It wasn't that he was tempted by exceptional pears; they were actually inferior to the pears he had at home. It's not even that it was time for a snack. Augustine and his companions didn't even eat the fruit they took; they threw it to the pigs.

Why, then, did he sin? Augustine tirelessly asks the question and relentlessly rejects one possible motivation after another. Finally, he asks if, perhaps, he found enjoyment in doing evil itself. But this, too, he dismisses as nonsense. No one, he says, commits evil for its own sake. No one chooses evil just because it's evil. People sin not for the sake of evil, but for the sake of something good.

Goodness Gracious

This is the part that scandalizes some Christians. How can he say that sinners do not choose evil when they sin? Augustine counters that human beings can only desire good things. We want what's sweet to the taste, what's comfortable, what makes us more free, what removes difficulties from our lives. Moreover, all the things we desire are good because God has created them that way. "And God saw everything that He had made, and behold, it was very good" (Gen 1:31). All the things in the world share, in some way, in God's glory. Every artwork bears the distinctive mark of its artist, so every creature is a manifestation of a natural sacrament of the creator. And it is that sample of divine glory that makes the things of this world so attractive to us.

What is it, then, that takes the desire for something good and transforms it into a sin? Augustine puts it beautifully: "Sins are committed when, out of an immoderate liking for things—since they are the least goods—we desert the best and highest goods," which are God, His truth, and His law. "These lower goods have their delights," he continues, "but none such as my God, Who has made all things; for in Him the just man finds delight, and He is the joy of the upright of heart."

Augustine concludes that he stole the pears for the sake of his friends' companionship and for the laughter they would share. The friendship, the camaraderie, and the laughter were all good things, gifts from God, and good to desire. Yet the boy went wrong when he placed the desire for these things before the desire to please and obey the Lord God.

We, too, sin not because we want what is evil, but because we want what isn't good enough. We give our hearts, our bodies, and our souls to trifles and passing sensations when we should go, instead, to the summit of all pleasures, the eternal creator of all joy. In fixating on God's gifts, we turn our backs to the giver.

A New, Whirled Order

The problem, then, is not that we find creatures attractive, but that we find them more attractive than God. The problem (in Augustine's words) is our "immoderate liking for things," for pleasure, and for earthly glory. This was the problem for Adam and Eve. For the forbidden fruit in Eden—like the fruit in Augustine's neighborhood orchard—was not evil. Indeed, the tree of the knowledge of good and evil was good in every way. Eve saw immediately "that the tree was good for food, and that it was a delight to the eyes, and that the tree was to be desired to make one wise" (Gen 3:6). The tree had all these natural good qualities because God had made it that way. It looked good, and it could do good, giving wisdom to the person who ate from it. But God had commanded the first couple to sacrifice all those great goods for the sake of a higher good, a supernatural good. And that is what they failed to do—out of fear of the serpent, out of pride, and out of a fear of suffering loss (see Heb 2:14–15). The fruit wasn't evil; but the disobedience certainly was. It's not bad to want knowledge, or to have a hankering for ripe apples, but it is bad to pursue these things in directions that lead away from God.

Adam and Eve did this. They reordered their priorities so that their immediate desires—safety, self-preservation, knowledge, and sensual delights—might be fulfilled, while the higher goods—such as faith, hope, and love—would be deferred. They did not directly choose evil. They chose lesser goods. They chose goods that seemed more *real* at the moment. Self-preservation and hunger are deep-seated animal instincts, for which the body produces intense physical responses. Yet there is no similar physical drive for faith, hope, and love. There is no gland, no organ, no hormone that will press us on to choose God above everything else. What was required of Adam and Eve was a sheer act of will—uniting their own will with God's will—and thus sacrificing all the lower desires of their bodies and souls, hearts and minds.

Their choice had long-term consequences. Their need created new needs: to hide themselves, to justify themselves, to cover their nakedness. Adam and Eve had given primary place to their lower desires, and now their lower desires were taking over. Whereas they had previously been "naked and unashamed," now their nakedness provoked disordered feelings in both of them; and they felt it necessary to cover up with garments woven from fig leaves. Whereas Adam had earlier tilled and kept the garden in a seemingly effortless way, now he found himself toiling in hardship and sweat.

Our first parents had reversed the divinely intended hierarchy in the human person and in the human race. Now, instead of our souls governing our bodies, our bodies—and their longings and appetites, pleasures and fears—were driving our souls.

Saint Paul calls this the rebellion of the flesh against the spirit (see Gal 5:16–17; Eph 2:3; *CCC*, n. 2515). Theologians call it *concupiscence* (pronounced *kon-KYOO-pi-sens*), a term that refers to our "human appetites or desires which remain disordered due to the temporal consequences of orginal sin." Concupiscence is by definition unreasonable: Our chaotic drives are in rebellion against the order of reason.

Concupiscence itself is not sin, but it is the result of original sin and the cause of actual sins. It is an innate inclination to sin; but it is not a personal transgression. Concupiscence does not render me guilty, but it does render me vulnerable to temptation and positively prone to sin.

Unsound Effects

"As by one man's disobedience many were made sinners, so by one man's obedience many will be made righteous" (Rom 5:19). As Adam snuffed out the divine life in his soul and the souls of his descendents, so Christ came to restore that divine life and enable us to share it. Most of us receive that divine life, when we are babies, through the sacrament of baptism.

Baptism takes away the stain of original sin, but concupiscence remains with us. Our drives and our passions, though good in themselves, are out of proper order, and that's *not* good.

Concupiscence is self-perpetuating, and it pulls us downward. We find creatures attractive because God made them that way, as samples of His glory, to lead us to thank Him, praise Him, and love Him all the more. But we tend to take these created things and make *them* the ultimate objects of our desire—whether a spouse or a friend, chocolate or alcohol, books or cars. The more we indulge our passionate desires, the more they take hold of us, and the more they increase our need for them. The more we need these created goods, the less we sense the need for God—even though it is He Who has given us the goods of the world!

Concupiscence renders us vulnerable, temptable. We are tempted by this world through our concupiscence. But just because we entertain thoughts that are wrong doesn't mean we're guilty. It isn't until we allow those thoughts to start entertaining us that we have committed an actual sin on the inside—and, unless we repent quickly, we will soon commit them on the outside.

In order to overcome the effects of concupiscence, we must first know what they are. Tradition names three.

1. Our intellects are darkened. Our faculty of reason now takes direction from our glands and our gut. It is only with God's grace, revealed truth, and our own effort that we can think past the promptings of our flesh.

2. Our wills are weakened. The will can only will the good. But the will acts upon the data provided by the intellect, which is now working in darkness. Thus our will is often misdirected—not toward God as our ultimate end, but toward creatures as our proximate end. The will still chooses good things; it just chooses lower goods, apparent goods. Nobody every chooses evil as evil, even the person committing suicide or murder. Hitler thought he was doing good by ridding the world of Jews, Gypsies, and Catholic priests.

That's how twisted human nature can become, once concupiscence is allowed free rein.

3. *Our appetites are disordered*. Our desire for food, sleep, sexual intimacy—all of these are good in themselves, when they are ordered to God, as they were created to be. But through concupiscence they become disorderly; and so our bodies have a tendency to drag us down into gluttony, laziness, lust, and other habitual sins.

You can see the ravages of concupiscence now. The intellect is darkened, so it is not feeding the will. Thus, the will is weakened further still. Finally, the desires of the flesh have become disorderly because the soul is no longer governing the body as it should.

Punished by Pleasure

By now we should better understand the cry of Saint Paul: "Wretched man that I am! Who will deliver me from this body of death?" (Rom 7:24). Like Paul, we should also be sure that our deliverance comes from Jesus Christ our Lord. We must, however, learn to discern Christ's call to repentance in our everyday lives, for these are the appointed moments of our deliverance.

Sin begins, for us, with our disordered desires. First we are tempted by a hankering after something we should not have. Our first level of obligation, then, is to resist temptation: to reject the desire and remove ourselves from the situation that is agitating us.

If we fail to do so and we sin, we have a graver and more difficult obligation, because we have placed ourselves in greater danger. We must now repent of our particular sin, confess it, and do penance for it.

But what if we don't repent? What if, instead, we go back for another round of the forbidden pleasure? Once we fail to fulfill the second level of obligation, then we face God's punishment. Even this, however, is not what we might expect. God doesn't ordinarily punish sinners by sending a lightning bolt from a sunny sky. The worst punishment we can receive is the attraction the sin exercises upon us. When people choose a forbidden pleasure, the punishment for sin becomes the pleasure they experience illicitly, because once they experience it, they want it more. If God abandons us to our illicit pleasures, we find we can no longer resist them at all. Before long, we're hooked. We're dependent, or co-dependent, or addicted.

Once we're hooked on a sin, our values are turned upside down. Evil becomes our most urgent "good," our deepest longing; what is actually good stands as an "evil" because it threatens to keep us from satisfying our illicit desires. At that point, repentance becomes almost impossible, because repentance is, by definition, a turning away from evil and toward the good; but, by now, the sinner has thoroughly redefined both good and evil. Isaiah said of such sinners: "Woe to those who call evil good and good evil" (Is 5:20).

Concupiscence run amok is God's punishment for unrepentant sin, and it's a punishment that fits the crime. When people persist in choosing the lesser good, God eventually removes their restraints. In the first chapter of his Letter to the Romans, Saint Paul explains that "God gave [the pagans] up in the lusts of their hearts to impurity . . . because they exchanged the truth about God for a lie and worshiped and served the creature rather than the creator" (Rom 1:24–25). "God gave them up to dishonorable passions" (1:26) and "to a base mind and to improper conduct" (1:28). In punishing people, God respects their freedom. He "gives them up" to the lusts, the passions, and the conduct that they themselves had chosen. But when God—Who gave them life—has given them up, can they be any more dead?

I'll say it again: The pleasure in sinning is the first punishment for sin. This comes as a surprise to most people. We think of divine punishment as a vendetta by which God gets even with sinners. But the worst temporal punishments God allows are the attachments that arise from sins freely chosen.

Drunks, for example, don't start off as drunks. They start off by getting drunk once, then again, then again. So if we desire alcohol and we don't moderate that desire, we find ourselves intoxicated; and the drunkenness is the punishment for the sin of immoderate drinking. At that point, we should realize that we have failed in our initial duty to resist temptation; we must then repent, confess, and do penance. But if we don't repent—if, instead, we go back for another drunken binge—then we will feel within our souls the weight of this illicit good drawing us downward, further away from God.

That's what happens when the intellect is darkened and the will weakened. We render ourselves almost incapable of repenting, apart from some divine intervention—a car wreck, abandonment by our family, eviction from our home, the loss of a job. When disaster strikes, the sinner usually thinks that God is finally waking up and beginning to punish him. But that is not divine wrath; it's divine mercy, saving the sinner from a worse and everlasting fate.

What we then see as punishments, as wrath, are really the flashes of sudden, brilliant light that God sends to illumine a soul darkened by concupiscence and sin.

Wrath as Metaphor, Wrath as Real

It is important that we come to understand God's punishments in the right way. The Old Testament speaks of God's "anger" or His "wrath" 168 times. Yet we can say with conviction that God does not "get angry"; He does not "punish" us in His "rage." For God is eternal and unchanging; thus, He does not undergo the movements and changes that human beings experience in our emotions and passions.

When the Bible speaks of God's "wrath," it is speaking metaphorically, as it often does. Think, for example, of the Psalmist's reference to God's "right hand and His holy arm" (Ps 98:1). This does not mean that God has limbs and members, any more than He has emotions and passions. Saint Thomas Aquinas explains: "When Scripture speaks of God's arm, the literal sense is not that God has such a member, but only what is signified by this member, namely operative power" (*Summa Theologica* 1.1.10 ad 3m).

What does the metaphor represent? *Anger* is a relational

word. If we are angry, we must have an object of our anger—someone with whom we're angry. Since *anger* cannot properly refer to something in the Trinity—for unchanging God has no eternal anger—it cannot refer to God's eternal relations. It must, then, speak of a temporal relationship between God and man. Saint Thomas is helpful here: "Thus with us it is usual for an angry man to punish, so that punishment becomes an expression of anger. Therefore punishment itself is signified by the word anger, when anger is attributed to God.... [Still,] anger is never attributed to God properly, since in its primary meaning it includes passion" (*Summa Theologica*, 1.19.11, c).

Divine *wrath*, *anger*, and *punishment* are terms that help us to understand the actions in our lives, and in history, by which God achieves justice and restores order. But these are not the ragings of a "hanging judge." They are, rather, the instrument of His mercy and kindness. God's punishments are like the chastisements of a loving father, or the press of the shepherd's rod and staff that guide us in right paths. They are remedial, restorative, redemptive, medicinal. Said Saint Paul: "God's kindness is meant to lead you to repentance" (Rom 2:4).

Truth and Consequences

God's anger has been defined as "the greatest disasters and blows which may strike people as the outcome of sin, as 'punishment' which is bound to sin because God has willed it." Saint Paul said: "We know that the judgment of God rightly falls upon those who do such things"—that is, who sin (Rom 2:2).

God often punishes us in ways we do not expect. But His punishments are never vindictive or arbitrary; they are the inevitable consequences of our free choices. Indeed, His punishments—even the ultimate and everlasting punishment of hell—are the very safeguards of human freedom and assurance of divine love. For no love can be coerced. We must be free to choose God's love or—tragically, ultimately—to reject it. If we did not have the option of choosing sin and hell, we could not have the freedom of truly choosing and loving God. If God did not permit us to say no to Him, our yes would be worthless, the programmed response of a machine.

We have to face the fact that when we sin and opt for something instead of God, we'll get what we choose.

Unfortunately, because we must make our choice using faculties weakened by concupiscence, it will always be a struggle. Concupiscence can only drag us in one direction: downward, away from God. Moreover, its gravity is overwhelming, overpowering us body and soul.

We can begin to overcome concupiscence through self-mastery and self-denial—indeed, we must do so—but even that is not enough. We need the help that only God can give: the grace He dispenses freely in the sacrament of penance. That grace works with divine and creative power; it *creates anew* the heart that sin has disordered, disfigured, and disgraced.

CHAPTER 7

THE THEMES FROM
DELIVERANCE:
CONFESSION AS COVENANT

W HO WILL DELIVER me from this body of death?" (Rom 7:24). Saint Paul gave voice to a cry that echoed through the millennia, from the time of the original sin. Those who had faith in God also had faith that God would "deliver" them, somehow, from the "law of sin and death" (Rom 7:2)—concupiscence—that ruled their bodies despotically.

Sacramental forgiveness is one powerful way we experience this long-awaited deliverance.

"Who will deliver me from this body of death?" Paul answered his own question without hesitation, knowing that God had sent Jesus as his deliverer. "Who will deliver me from this body of death?" (Rom 7:24). "Christ Jesus has set me free from the law of sin and death" (Rom 7:2). "Thanks be to God through Jesus Christ our Lord!" (Rom 7:25).

What form did this deliverance take? Scripture and Christian Tradition use an array of terms for the event and the fact. They speak of *atonement, redemption, salvation, justifi-*

cation, and *sanctification,* among other terms. Most Christians, perhaps, treat these words as interchangeable synonyms. The words are at once overly familiar to us, from their repetition in prayers and pious phrases, and yet unfamiliar to us in relation to everyday, workaday reality. For the average Christian, these words mean little apart from their religious context. Thus, the mind tends to tune out whenever the Latinate syllables start piling up.

Those who take the time to ponder each term are sometimes little better off. For the words represent a jumble of realities that seem to be in mutual conflict or contradiction: military, religious, mercantile, legal. Our deliverance begins to look like a most improbable mix of metaphors.

Yet it was not that way to those who first experienced their deliverance. It was not that way to Saint Paul, for whom all those metaphors represented a single unitary experience. It was an experience common to him, to the other apostles, to Jesus, to their ancestors in Israel, and to their neighbors in the ancient world.

God always explains what is unknown in terms of what is known. And all those terms—*redemption, salvation, justification, sanctification*—come together in a single reality that was known throughout the ancient Church and ancient Israel. They came together in the notion of *covenant.*

Pact House

To understand the notion of covenant, we must first understand the culture of ancient Israel, in which the large, extended family defined the world of a given individual. The family—the tribe, the clan—constituted a man or woman's primary identity, dictating where they would live, how they would work, and whom they might marry. Often, people wore a conspicuous sign of their family identity, such as a signet ring or a distinguishing mark on the body.

A nation in the ancient Near East was largely a network of such families, as Israel comprised the twelve tribes named for Jacob's sons. Unifying each family was the bond of covenant, with all its attendant rights, duties, and loyalties. When a family welcomed new members through marriage, adoption, or some other alliance, both parties—the new members and the established tribe—would seal the covenant bond, usually by solemnly swearing a sacred oath, sharing a common meal, and offering a sacrifice. The great biblical scholar Dennis J. McCarthy, S.J., wrote: "There is no doubt that covenants, even treaties, were thought of as establishing a kind of quasi-familial unity. In the technical vocabulary of these documents, a superior partner was called 'father,' his inferior 'son,' and equal partners were 'brothers.' "

Each of these extended families was an economic unit. Indeed, it was literally an economy. The word *economy* comes from the Greek *oikonomia,* meaning "law of the household." The marketplace, with its buying and selling, was a family matter. A man's profession was not so much a matter of personal choice as of family need.

Each extended family was a military unit. The family looked after its own and was prepared to defend its people, its land, and its trade. If a family member was endangered in any way, the family would dispatch a kinsman-redeemer—in Hebrew, *go 'el*—to rescue the victim or avenge the crime (see Gen 14:14–16).

Each extended family was a religious unit. The family was united in its profession of religion and its practice of sacrifice. Fathers functioned in a priestly role, offering sacrifice for their family, and passed the office on to their firstborn sons. The family's god was the god of their ancestors, the patriarchs: "The God of Abraham and of Isaac and of Jacob, the God of our fathers" (Acts 3:13).

Each extended family was governed by its own courts. The family tended to adjudicate its own disputes and prosecute crimes committed by its members, against its members, or on its lands. The tribal elders served as judges (see Ex 18:21–26; Dt 1:12–17; and Dt 21:19).

In Other Words

God's relationship with His chosen people was defined by a covenant. So the Scripture often describes their interaction, as we might expect, in familial terms. But, by *familial,* we must also include the range of activities described above: the economic, military, religious, and juridical. Thus, we come to the vocabulary used for God's deliverance.

Economic. Deliverance here finds expression in the language of the marketplace: "You were bought with a price" (1 Cor 7:23). The word can also describe the purchase of a slave or the ransom of a captive. The New Testament uses it in this way, but with a familial twist: "God sent forth His

Son, born of woman, born under the law, to redeem those who were under the law, so that we might receive adoption as sons" (Gal 4:4–5). Saint Paul also connects redemption with the forgiveness of sins and the healing of concupiscence: "Our great God and Savior Jesus Christ . . . gave Himself for us to redeem us from all iniquity and to purify for Himself a people of His own who are zealous for good deeds" (Tit 2:13–14).

Military. Sometimes, Scripture portrays our deliverance in battlefield terminology: the kinsman-avenger liberating his people from their captors or enemies. In the definitive act of rescue, Jesus saves us from sin: "The Lord will rescue me from every evil and save me for His heavenly kingdom" (2 Tim 4:18). We hear echoes of this also in the Lord's Prayer, where Jesus taught us to pray: "deliver us from the evil one" (Mt 6:13). The theme appears, later, in Ephesians (6:10–17), in which Paul speaks at length of spiritual warfare and our need to "put on the armor of God" (see also Is 59:15–21).

Religious (or Liturgical). The word literally refers to the act of making holy. In the Old Testament, we find it used to describe the purification rites connected with the Jerusalem Temple and its priestly sacrifice. Men and women purified themselves in preparation for the Temple sacrifice, and they were in turn made purer by the Temple sacrifice. In the New Testament, it is the sacrifice of Jesus Christ—mediated through the sacraments—that purifies the Church and its members: "They have washed their robes and made them white in the blood of the Lamb" (Rev 7:14). "But you were washed, you were sanctified, you were justified in the name of the Lord Jesus Christ and in the Spirit of our God" (1 Cor 6:11). Our purification, our sanctification, come about through our baptism.

Juridical. Here we see salvation described in legal terms, as exoneration of our many sins before God as our judge. This, too, is the work of Jesus Christ, Who won our acquittal by enabling us to share His own blameless life. "They are justified by His grace as a gift, through the redemption which is in Christ Jesus" (Rom 3:24). "And the free gift is not like the effect of [Adam's] sin. For the judgment following one trespass brought condemnation, but the free gift following many trespasses brings justification. If, because of one man's trespass, death reigned through that one man, much more will those who receive the abundance of grace and the free gift of righteousness reign in life through the one man Jesus Christ" (Rom 5:16–17).

Substitute Teaching

Redemption, salvation, sanctification, justification—while all those terms can deliver God's saving word, we need to rediscover how they converge in the single reality of the covenant.

No scholar or serious reader of the Bible denies that the covenant was a central idea—indeed, *the* central idea—in ancient Israel. Everyone accepts the word; we're less certain, however, about what the word represents. We are so far away in time and space that it's difficult for us to overcome the conceptual distance. It is arduous for us to reconstruct what seemed so natural to the biblical writers, but which now seems unnatural to us.

However, when we begin to piece together the Israelite

experience of covenant, we soon find ourselves describing the lived reality in those four sets of terms: *military*, *mercantile*, *legal*, and *liturgical*. And this is not merely a historical curiosity. For when we apply our historical findings to theological reasoning, we discover that Catholic theology offers much to remedy what is lacking in the work of many non-Catholic preachers. Listen to the TV and radio sermons of many evangelists, and soon you'll pick up certain commonplaces: for example, that God punished our sin in Christ; that the Father no longer saw His only begotten Son, but only our sin, and so He vented His wrath upon Jesus. Then—according to this reading—the legal exchange was complete. Jesus took on our guilt and punishment, and we received His righteousness and reward.

Mutual Savings

The problem with that legal exchange is that it's a legal fiction, a false exchange. Jesus wasn't guilty of the crime, and so He really could not be punished for it. The legal conventions in Israel were similar to those we know today. If I were to damage someone's property and be found guilty in small-claims court, my neighbor would be able to step in and pay a debt that I could not afford. Economic damages could be transferred or exchanged—but not criminal penalties. If I were found guilty of murder, the same neighbor could not step forward to be executed or incarcerated on my behalf. Criminal penalties, then as now, could not be borne by substitutes.

If Christ *had* merely served as our substitute, we might

rightly ask why we still have to bear the punishment for our sins: Why must we still suffer and die? As our substitute, Christ should have eliminated the need for our suffering.

But, according to the logic of the covenant—and the teaching of the Church—He was not our penal substitute. He was, rather, our legal representative; and, since His saving passion was representative, it doesn't exempt us from suffering, but rather endows our suffering with divine power and redemptive value (see Col 1:24).

Yes, we affirm that Jesus paid a debt He did not owe (because we owed a debt we couldn't pay). Economically, the substitutionary theory works; but in criminal law, it does not. For an innocent man to be punished in our place would itself be a kind of injustice. That itself would indicate a divine blindness or temporary madness. How, after all, could the Father "not see" His only Son, especially at the moment when the Son is hanging there out of total obedience and love for the Father? Of course, the Father *could* see the Son, and never was the humanity of Christ so beautiful as when He hung on the cross in loving submission to the will of the Father!

Such preaching—of a blind Father visiting vengeance upon an innocent Son—is unacceptable and borders on blasphemy. It demands to be corrected and completed by the one principle that verifies all the metaphors for God's saving action.

We need to know the covenant. But in order to understand it, we first need to step on tiptoe and peer over the wall of our culture and see what made the Gospel so sensible for first-century Christians. It was the covenant-family understood in legal terms, as well as liturgical, economic, and military. This was the understanding in the natural, tribal family of Israel. It's the understanding today in the sacramental, universal family of the Church, where we experience spiritual warfare, redemptive work and suffering, ritual worship, and a court at which we plead guilty and seek mercy: the sacrament of confession.

Rite Turns

Christ came to fulfill the ancient covenants in every way. Thus we see every aspect of Old Testament family life come to full flower in the New.

In His covenants with Adam, Noah, Abraham, Moses, and David, God opened membership in His covenant family to ever more people: first to a married couple, then to a household, then to a tribe, then to a nation, then to a kingdom—till, finally, the invitation was made universal with Jesus. Christ's "true family" consists of those who receive new birth as children of God through baptism (Jn 3:3–8), and who continue to share His life through the sacraments. They become His younger brothers (see Rom 8:14–15,29).

The sacraments are now the means by which men and women are incorporated into God's covenant family. The sacraments also serve to renew the covenant and to restore it when it has been broken.

Sacraments mark the Christian's covenant oath, common meal, and sacrifice. The word *sacrament* itself witnesses to this truth. As I said previously, the word *sacrament* comes from the Latin *sacramentum*, which means "oath," and the word was applied to the Church's rites from the earliest days. The pagan Roman historian Pliny the Younger recorded (around A.D. 110) that Christians of his day would gather before sunrise to sing hymns to Christ, after which they would "bind themselves by a solemn oath . . . never to commit any fraud, theft, or adultery, never to falsify their word." Pliny went on to say that after swearing this *sacramentum,* the Christians would disperse, then reassemble later on to receive the Eucharist.

It sounds much like the "confession" before Communion recorded earlier, in the mid-first-century *Didache*. Indeed, it sounds very much like the sort of confession that Jesus prescribed as the proper prerequisite to our sharing in His sacrifice: "If you are offering your gift at the altar, and there remember that your brother has something against you, leave your gift there before the altar and go; first be reconciled to your brother, and then come and offer your gift" (Mt 5:23–24).

To be "reconciled to your brother"—in the sight of your Father God—is to be fully restored to the family. And that family bond is what God restores to Christians in the sacrament of confession. Confession restores us to brotherhood and sisterhood within the Church, which is the family of God on earth; and it restores us as children of God, in Christ, in the eternal Family of God in heaven.

Once reconciled, we can, with pure hearts, return to the altar of sacrifice. There we can receive the blood of the new and everlasting covenant—the blood of Christ, by which we are ransomed, and justified, and sanctified, and saved.

The Son Set

Forgiveness is a great gift, but it's a penultimate gift. It's intended to prepare us for something still greater. Christians are saved not only *from* sin, but *for* sonship—divine sonship in Christ. We are not just criminals who have been exonerated; we are sons and daughters who have been adopted. We are children of God, "sons in the Son," and we share the life of the Trinity.

We are indeed forgiven by God's grace, but not merely forgiven; we are adopted and divinized. That is, we "become partakers of the divine nature" (2 Pet 1:4). This is ultimately why God created man, to share in the life-giving love of the Trinity. Self-sacrificial love is the essential law of God's covenant, which man broke but Jesus kept. Through the incarnation, God transformed human nature into a perfect image—and instrument—of the Trinity's love, by offering it as a sacrificial gift-of-self to the Father on our behalf. The Son of God "took the form of a servant" (Phil 2:6) so that sinful servants may be restored as sons of God. As Saint Athanasius declared: "The Son of God became the Son of Man so that sons of men could become sons of God."

The essential effect of confession, then, is enabling our forgiveness so that we can be restored to Trinitarian life. As adopted children, Christians can "call God 'Father,' in union with the only Son" (*CCC*, n. 1997).

CHAPTER 8

CLEARING THE HEIR:
SECRETS OF THE PRODIGAL SON

CONFESSION IS A family affair. It's a family reunion. It's the return of a wayward child to the family home and the Father's arms.

For Christians throughout history, the sacrament has been more than a doctrine. It's a story—the story of a falling and a rising, estrangement and reconciliation. It is the story of everyone's own life. But whenever Christians talk about the sacrament, they inevitably speak of it, just as Jesus did, in terms of a *particular* story, a family story. That story is the parable of the prodigal son (Lk 15:11–32).

A Wayward Son Carries On

Jesus tells us of a rich man who had two sons. The younger son asked if he could have his share of his inheritance now, rather than waiting till his father's death, and the father granted his wish. The young son promptly packed up and traveled to a far country, where he squandered his property in loose living. And when he had spent everything, his personal bankruptcy coincided with a natural disaster. A famine came. So he took a job feeding pigs. The young man was so hungry, he would have gladly eaten the pigs' food, but no one offered him anything.

At last he came to his senses and thought: "How many of my father's hired servants have bread enough and to spare, but I perish here with hunger! I will arise and go to my father, and I will say to him, 'Father, I have sinned against heaven and before you; I am no longer worthy to be called your son; treat me as one of your hired servants.' "

So he started the long journey back home. While he was still some distance away, his father spotted him. Overwhelmed by compassion, the father ran down the road, embraced his son, and kissed him.

And the son began the speech he had rehearsed: "Father, I have sinned against heaven and before you; I am no longer worthy to be called your son . . ." But his father would not let him finish. Instead, the old man turned to his servants, saying, "Bring quickly the best robe, and put it on him; and put a ring on his hand, and shoes on his feet; and bring the fatted calf and kill it, and let us eat and make merry; for this my son was dead, and is alive again; he was lost, and is found." And then the feast began.

Meanwhile, the elder son was coming in from work in the fields; as he approached the house, he heard music and dancing. He called one of the servants and asked what was going on. The servant explained everything, while the brother became furious. He refused to go in.

The father came out and pleaded with him. But the elder son answered, "Lo, these many years I have served you, and I never disobeyed your command; yet you never gave me a kid, that I might make merry with my friends. But when this son of yours came, who has devoured your living with harlots, you killed for him the fatted calf!"

The father replied, "Son, you are always with me, and all that is mine is yours. It was fitting to make merry and be glad, for this your brother was dead, and is alive; he was lost, and is found."

Same Old Story?

Believers have meditated on that story and marveled over it for two millennia. Poets have sung about it. The greatest artists have tried to capture it on canvas, in marble, and in stained glass. Preachers have pondered it often and thundered its message from their pulpits. The story has been retold, retooled, revised, and expanded in novels, short stories, TV shows, and movies. The parable of the prodigal son is probably one of three or four most familiar stories in the world.

For that very reason, however, we should take a moment here, pause, and study it more closely, in its context, and in its small details. For we can become too familiar with a story. We can become so familiar that we filter out all but the familiar moments. We don't hear words; we see pictures as we conjured them up years ago, or as we remember them from our illustrated family Bible. We skip ahead, then, to the conclusions we made when we first "figured it out" or had a preacher spell out its meaning for us. A familiar story is one we assume we don't have to think about.

With some stories, perhaps, that's true, but not with the parables of Jesus Christ. For His stories come from the same divine genius that fashioned the universe out of nothing. God wrote the world the way human authors write books. So when He puts His mind to a story, you can bet that its meaning, like the world's, will be inexhaustible.

With this story, we need to step back and consider the bigger picture. We need to look at the story as Jesus told it and Saint Luke reported it, in its literary, historical, and cultural context.

All four of the gospels are rich in material about mercy, but none so much as Luke's. Only Luke tells us of the "good thief" who, after a lifetime of sin, wins his place in paradise with his dying breath, hanging next to Jesus on a cross (see Lk 23:39–43). When Luke shows us Jesus' telling the prodigal son story, it comes in a section thick with parables—earthly stories with heavenly meanings—and most of those stories deal, in some sense, with mercy.

What the Pharisee Saw

What triggers Jesus' extended teaching on mercy? The immediate context is the pharisees' grumbling about Jesus. They are outraged that he would sit down and eat meals with disreputable men. "Now the tax collectors and sinners were all drawing near to hear Jesus. And the pharisees and the scribes murmured, saying, 'This man receives sinners and eats with them' " (Lk 15:1–2). It wasn't the first time they had raised this complaint. On another occasion, Jesus had answered them shortly and sharply: "Those who are well have no need of a physician, but those who are sick; I have not come to call the righteous, but sinners to repentance" (see Lk 5:30–32). But apparently they had not accepted His answer.

Jesus and the pharisees were alike in one sense: Both considered table fellowship to be extremely important. For all pious Jews, ordinary meals held religious significance and were governed by certain liturgical rubrics. There were blessings along with the ritual breaking of bread and perhaps the sharing of a cup of wine. The very idea of "fast food" would seem blasphemous to them.

The pharisees observed these traditions scrupulously. They would not permit their meals to be profaned by the presence of sinners, Gentiles, or others who were considered "unclean" (menstruating women, for example, or anyone who had touched a corpse). Such exclusivity was essential, not incidental, to the pharisees' identity. Of all the traditions of the ancient schools of the pharisees Hillel and Shammai, 67 percent deal with table fellowship and purity. The very name *pharisee* was derived from the Hebrew word *parushim*, which means "the separated ones." They held themselves aloof from the rabble with whom Jesus was eating His meals.

Jesus, on the other hand, seemed to delight in the sort of people who made up the "great multitudes" that kept His company (Lk 14:25). He spoke metaphorically in terms of a rich man who planned a feast but who was spurned by all the "better" sort of people—the landowners, professionals, and merchants—and so told his servants to bring in society's outcasts: "Go out to the highways and hedges, and compel people to come in, that my house may be filled" (Lk 14:23).

Lost and Found

The pharisees murmured, "This man receives sinners and eats with them!"

Since simple and direct answers didn't seem to work, Jesus responded this time, in the fifteenth chapter of Luke's gospel, by telling three stories: the parable of the lost sheep, the parable of the lost coin, and the parable of the lost son. This last is better known as the parable of the prodigal son.

In each parable, the lost possession is something valuable. Consider the lost sheep. In the lands where Jesus preached, the people depended upon sheep for wool, for food, and for ritual sacrifice. To a herdsman, a single lost sheep meant lost income over the course of several years. Thus, the shepherd leaves his ninety-nine to fetch the single stray. Consider, too, the "lost coin." It was a drachma, a day's wages for an able-bodied man. Women had far less economic clout, and so a lost drachma might mean days without meals for the story's heroine.

But who could place a value on the lost son?

The story of the prodigal son begins with a family: a father and his two sons. The three are united by bonds of blood, but even more by bonds of covenant. It is the order of the covenant—the logic of the covenant—that undergirds the parable and shapes the drama.

A father could never set a price for his son. The youth, however, was willing to sell himself cheaply—though he thought the price quite extravagant. He asked if he could draw immediately on his portion of the family estate. This was an odd request. It was considered unusual and even shameful for a son to demand his inheritance in advance—as if he were impatient for his father's demise. The Book of Sirach, written shortly before Jesus' lifetime, set the proper time for bestowing an inheritance: "At the time when you end the days of your life, in the hour of death, distribute your inheritance" (Sir 33:23). A son who rushed the day would seem disrespectful, at the least.

The father, however, fulfilled his son's request, and the boy proceeded to behave as if his father were indeed dead and gone. The prodigal son wasted no time in packing and leaving his family behind. We must not miss the significance of his "journey into a far country" (Lk 15:13). In leaving behind the family lands, he was placing himself outside the covenant, abandoning the customs of his people, forsaking the God of his fathers. He was choosing to live as a Gentile.

His subsequent behavior bore this out. Jesus sums it up as "loose living" (Lk 15:13). With no father to watch over him, the youth indulged his already disordered desires, which became still more debased. His older brother lets us know that prostitutes were the primary beneficiaries of the young man's prodigality (Lk 15:30).

The younger son's moral bankruptcy arrived well in advance of his financial ruin, which came just as famine struck his country of residence. After months of indulging every whim, he now could not even fulfill his basic bodily needs. He was starving. So he took the only job available to him—and it was the most demeaning job a Jew could imagine. He worked as a swineherd, a keeper of the most unclean of animals (see Lev 11:17). Working for a Gentile employer, he would be expected to violate the weekly Sabbath as well (see Ex 20:8–11). Only the most desperate conditions would force the son to take this disgraceful position.

Moreover, he discovered that his own lot was much worse than that of the pigs. They, at least, were fed at regular intervals. No one displayed a similar concern for his nourishment. He found himself pining for the husks and pods that he threw to the herd; but none were forthcoming.

Homeward Bound

Previously, I said that the young man's moral and financial ruin "coincided" with the natural disaster of a famine. I do not mean, however, that this was a chance occurrence. It was coincident, simultaneous, but it was no accident. Indeed, I'd say it was provident. For only such a catastrophe could have brought about the prodigal son's conversion. It wasn't a warm wave of nostalgia that set him on the road to his father's house. It was hunger, shame, and the fear of death. As he came to his senses, he realized that it would be better to live as a slave to his father than to die, in a foreign land, as a slave to his sensuality. While he ached for a taste of pig fodder, the lowliest servants back home had "bread enough and to spare" (Lk 15:17).

So he began his return, and surely the long journey seemed longer still on an empty stomach. By the time he stood in sight of his father's lands, his hunger and shame must have been as overpowering as his odor.

His father sighted him from afar. How could that be so if he had not been always on the lookout for his lost son?

The old man then does something remarkable. He runs down the road to greet his boy. This was just short of a cultural taboo. It was considered unseemly for a nobleman to run. But this patriarch put aside his greatness and dignity to greet his son and lavish his love upon him. He embraces his son—the Greek phrase is more evocative: he "fell upon his neck" (Lk 15:20).

The son began to give voice to his prepared speech, but after a few words the father had heard enough. "Father, I have sinned against heaven and before you." The son's contrition was imperfect, just a little more than a hankering after a full belly and a warm bed, but it was enough. For he had come to his home and he had acknowledged his sin.

The third-century commentator Origen notes that it was only after the son had shown some small contrition— only after he had made his confession—that the father brought him home. "He would not add the sin 'against heaven' if he did not believe that heaven is his fatherland,

and that he did wrong when he left it. So, such a confession makes his father well disposed to him."

Then, quite suddenly, a sin that had been mortal—a sin that had killed off the boy's sonship, his inheritance, and his family life—was instantly forgiven, absolved, taken away: "for this my son was dead, and is alive again" (Lk 15:24).

A Ringing Endorsement

It is a remarkable story—just a few lines, really, in the gospel. Yet everything is there: the law of sin, the downward spiral of concupiscence, the ever more darkened intellect; the mortality of grave sin, the moral "death" of the son; the severe mercy of God's providence, the disasters; and God's readiness to come out and meet sinners partway while they're still on the road to true contrition.

What does the son receive upon being reconciled with his father? The "best robe," a ring for his hand, shoes for his feet, and a banquet in his honor (Lk 15:22–23). Each of these gifts has enormous symbolic value. The signet ring is the emblem of the covenant family, to which the son is restored. Along with the robe, it is a sign of his share in his father's authority. (For striking Old Testament parallels, see Gen 41:42; Es 3:10; 1 Mac 6:15.) The shoes are the distinctive mark of a free man. Household slaves normally went about barefoot. Though the son chose to be a slave to his passions, and then to pagan masters—and though he begged to be made a slave on his ancestral lands—his father will have none of that. The youth was not set free from pagan slavery merely to enjoy a better sort of slavery. He was saved for sonship; and if he is a son, then he is an heir, sharing in his father's authority.

But first he must share his father's life, and so share his table! The narrative moves from the road to the banquet hall, from confession to feast, from estrangement to table fellowship. The Greek word most commonly used for such fellowship is *koinonia*, which we sometimes translate as "communion." The father restores the son to communion in the place where everyone has "bread enough and to spare."

Of the prodigal father, what can we say? Without hesitation: "This man receives sinners and eats with them!"

Big Brother Is Watching

We must not, however, forget that there is a third character in this drama. And if Jesus' parable is directed primarily to the pharisees, then this character is perhaps the most important of all. I believe he is, and I have often called this story the parable of the elder brother.

For the older brother's attitude reflects the bitterness of the pharisees (Lk 15:2), who wrongly saw God's acceptance of sinners as a violation of covenant justice. Think for a moment about the classic formula of a covenant oath:

> I call heaven and earth to witness against you this day, that
> I have set before you life and death, blessing and curse;
> therefore choose life, that you and your descendants may

live, loving the Lord your God, obeying His voice, and cleaving to Him; for that means life to you and length of days, that you may dwell in the land which the Lord swore to your fathers. (Dt 30:19–20)

Sinners are those who, by definition, have violated their covenant oath, transgressed the law, chosen death, chosen the curse, and forfeited their right to live in the fatherland as sons and heirs. The prodigal son is by this definition a great sinner who has merited the full force of the curse.

The older brother, like the pharisees, rages with resentment against a perceived injustice; and he, like the pharisees, does not begin to understand the logic of covenant love.

Indeed, there are consequences that must follow upon the violation of a covenant. But there is also a way to come home again. The covenant is a family bond, not a bill of slavery. A broken covenant can be restored and renewed.

The problem with the older brother (as with the pharisees) is that he does not think in terms of the family, but in terms of slavery. His speech betrays him. Though he has been constant in his labors, he works with the joyless attitude of a slave, merely obeying the "commands" of his master (Lk 15:29). Unlike his younger sibling, he never addresses the old man as "Father," but "you." Nor does the firstborn ever refer to junior as "brother," just "this son of yours" (Lk 15:30). Even in his jealousy of his little brother's feast, big brother does not wish for a family dinner, but a party with his buddies—"a kid, that I might make merry with my friends" (Lk 15:29). This is the rhetoric of slavery, not sonship.

Perpetual Problem

Jesus addressed His parable to certain individuals who stood before Him. They were pharisees who wanted to take a law already impossible to fulfill and make it even more difficult. He surely did not intend the story to be anti-Jewish, as some critics have charged; for Jesus Himself was an observant Jew who praised the enduring power of the law of Moses (see Mt 5:18).

The problem, moreover, is not peculiar to older brothers, or to pharisees, or to any particular religious group. It's our problem. It belongs to every age and people. It is a recurring sin among the just that they take pride in their righteousness; they claim credit for their good deeds; and they wish to impose a corresponding obligation on God. It is a perversion of the covenant, and it has been as pervasive under the New Covenant as under the Old.

Most of the heresies that the Church has suffered were errors of hyperpurity, not hyperlaxity. In the third century, the Montanists were scandalized by the slack behavior of some clergy, and so they set themselves apart; they separated themselves from the sinners. A short time later, the Donatists judged the Church too lenient in readmitting traitors. They decided to hold their own Eucharist, by invitation only. All these purer-than-thou heresies (and many more) found scandal in the Church's desire to "receive sinners and eat with them." Instead of an ever greater communion, they chose the path of separatism, exclusivism, and division—the path chosen by those long-ago pharisees.

The Church, like Christ, could not accommodate this doctrine. That is the reason why we Catholics profess, in the words of the ancient creeds, our belief in "the forgiveness of sins." We profess it because there are always some people who will deny it.

No Fear

The drama of the parable moves from slavery to sonship, from excommunication to table fellowship, from confession to communion. The father put aside his greatness and dignity and humbled himself to share in his son's condition, so that his son might once again share an exalted life in the family. This was the way of the prodigal father. It was the way of God Himself, Who became incarnate so that man might become deified: "May we come to share in the divinity of Christ, Who humbled Himself to share in our humanity."

This is not just a story of long ago and far away. It is our story, as it was the story of Saint Paul, who wrote what could have been a commentary on Jesus' parable: "For you did not receive the spirit of slavery to fall back into fear, but you have received the spirit of sonship. When we cry, 'Abba! Father!' it is the Spirit Himself bearing witness with our spirit that we are children of God, and if children, then heirs, heirs of God and fellow heirs with Christ" (Rom 8:15–17).

God continues to meet us halfway on the road to repentance. He met us once for all in His incarnation. He meets us even now in the confessional, so that He might guide us to His table, where there is the Bread of Life—"bread enough and to spare."

CHAPTER 9

EXILES ON MAIN STREET: NO TRUE HOME AWAY FROM HOME

E ACH OF US is God's prodigal child. We run away from home, and we misspend the gifts that our Father has lavished upon us. In our choices, we prefer the enticements of a foreign land to the love and freedom that children enjoy in the household of their parents. All this takes place whenever we sin. We return to our Father whenever we return to the sacrament of penance.

Yet, inevitably, we sin again, and we come home again. Unlike the prodigal son, we will not know our *definitive* homecoming until the moment of our death—which, ideally, should come soon after our last confession.

Till that moment, we must live our lives as if in "a far country"—distant from our true home—a strange country, delightful to the senses, and full of good things. It is so delightful, in fact, that it could make us forget our homeland.

Again, we are like the prodigal son. It is by our Father's kindness that we may visit this country. We could not have gotten here without His riches to pay the way. We could not survive here without our share of His fortune. For God created the world where we live as strangers, and He sustains it in existence; and He created us, too.

We must live in this world, then, as good children of our Father, even though we are far from home and our Father will not compel us to do so.

Sojourners' Truth

Throughout their life on earth, Christians live as if in exile from heaven. An anonymous Christian of the second century put it this way: "Inhabiting Greek as well as barbarian cities . . . they follow the customs of the natives in respect to clothing, food, and the rest of their ordinary conduct. . . . They dwell in their own countries, but simply as sojourners. As citizens, they share in all things with others, and yet endure all things as if foreigners. Every foreign land is like a native country to them, and every land of their birth is like a land of strangers" (Epistle to Diognetus 5).

God made us for heaven, but He made us on earth. For now, heaven is separated from us not by light-years of space, but by our sins. We will not know the comforts of our heavenly home until we come faithfully to the end of our estrangement and are purged of our sins. Till that day, we live, to one degree or another, in exile.

Even so, God our Father has created our place of exile, and it's a good place. Indeed, He made the world so that its delights—although they can never quite satisfy us—will remind us of our true home in heaven. All earthly goods are mere samples of heavenly perfections. The spiritual writer Father John Hugo put it this way:

> The beauty, the goodness, the truth, every excellence contained in creatures is . . . infinitely multiplied in the boundless goodness of God. . . . We glorify God through creatures when we see them as samples or rays of the divine beauty and goodness, and therefore a stairway and means to approaching God and loving Him, the source of all created good. Thereafter this love of God the supreme good embraces all the creatures that we use or touch or handle. . . . [W]e do not seek them as our final goal, we do not place our happiness in them, yet they become a means of loving Him Who is our true and final good, our joy, and our real fulfillment.

God designed the things of this world so that, by their inability to satisfy us, they should impel us ever more toward heaven.

They should, but they don't *necessarily*. For we are men and women and not beasts or trees. The achievement of our final goal does not come instinctively to us, as it does for squirrels, lions, and dogs—or inexorably, as it does for volcanoes, continents, and stars. Reason and nature might indicate what's best for us. But we are still free to choose otherwise. A doctor or confessor might tell us clearly and explicitly what we need to do. But we may still do something else. We must choose the good freely. And there remains the matter of our own will and intellect, which are wounded by concupiscence.

The delights of this world have a power to bewitch us. Rightly ordered, they should whet our appetite for God. But, because of concupiscence, we tend to develop disordered appetites for the earthly goods themselves. We want more of them than we really need. We become addicted to them. Soon, we would choose them instead of what is truly good for us. We would rather sin than leave an earthly desire unfulfilled.

The classic definition of sin is "a turning away from God and turning toward creatures." It's not that creatures are bad; in fact, they're very good, since they were created by God. We choose badly, however, when we decide to enjoy creatures rather than to love God, do His will, and follow His commandments. To put a creature in God's place is what our ancestors meant by the word *idolatry*. All sin is, in some sense, a form of idolatry: to prefer the creature to the creator, the gift to the giver.

This world is so delightful that it's easy for us to "go for the gusto" in our fleeting earthly moments and to forget our eternal destiny. We forget that we are exiles, far from home, and we wish we could just settle down comfortably in this land—no matter what our new citizenship might cost us.

Walk Like an Egyptian?

It is no accident that the plot of salvation history turns most often on stories of exodus, exile, pilgrimage, and aimless wandering. Adam and Eve got themselves expelled from the Garden of Eden (Gen 3:23–24). As a consequence of his fratricide, Cain had to leave his homeland and live in fear in the Land of Wandering (Gen 4:12–14). For the sins of the world, Noah had to put out in a boat while waters deluged all lands (Gen 9). The citizens of Babel rose up in pride against the Lord God, who "scattered them abroad from there over the face of all the earth" (Gen 11:8). Abraham dwelt in prosperity in Ur of the Chaldeans till God called him to make an improbable journey to a distant land (Gen 12:1).

God's people are always *en route*. There is no standing still in their earthly life. They (and we) are either progressing on pilgrimage toward God and toward His promised land, or drifting, wandering, or fleeing elsewhere.

The early Christians saw these historical events as symbols, or "types," of spiritual realities. The Israelites' enslavement in Egypt represented the state of humanity in bondage to original sin. The Israelites could not break free through their own efforts. God had to deliver them miraculously. And, even then, the chosen people had to subdue many enemies, without and within. For, over the course of 430 years (see Ex 12:40), even the best of the Israelites had assimilated too well to Egyptian culture. They had developed habits of mind, body, and spirit that had to be overcome. That is one reason why God commanded them to sacrifice certain animals—the very animals that pagan Egypt considered divine. The Israelites' sacrifices were a violent repudiation of their former infidelities to God, when they had adopted their captors' superstitions. God knew that habits developed over centuries could only be eradicated with difficulty. Thus He imposed upon Israel a demanding law, an all-encompassing regimen that minutely prescribed new customs for diet, hygiene, sex, and worship.

The new way was difficult for the chosen people; indeed, to many, the years of wandering in the desert seemed far worse than the centuries of oppression and forced labor. They grew nostalgic for the time of slavery, when at least their bellies had been full. "Who will give us meat to eat? For it was well with us in Egypt. . . . Why did we come forth out of Egypt?" (Num 11:18, 20).

Un-Bull-Leaving Israelites

And it wasn't only their bellies that were groaning after their departure from Egypt. They also built a golden image of Apis, a bull calf, the Egyptian god of virility, and they conducted an orgy there in the desert (Ex 32:1–6).

Israel was its own worst enemy, but certainly not its only one. On the way to their occupation of the promised land, the Israelites had to conquer seven mighty nations that opposed their advance.

All of this, according to the fathers of the Church, is like the situation of humanity. We are born slaves. That is why Israel's servile stint with Egypt is a typological picture of the soul in original sin. It's also why Israel being led through the Red Sea is a symbol of baptism (see 1 Cor 10:1–4). God has set us free, through baptism, from the slavery of original sin, but we still suffer its aftereffects in lingering concupiscence. So it is only with difficulty that we give up sinful habits. Moreover, our corrupt nature continues to hanker after the sensual pleasures that accompany a life of slavery to sin. If we are to break free of the land of our exile, we must put to death such longings—our concupiscence. We must sacrifice, in our lives, the created things that sinners tend to make into idols.

We need to discipline ourselves to resist temptation. We need to train ourselves to make war against the world, the concupiscent flesh, and the devil. The fathers of the Church pointed out that, like the Israelites, we, too, must conquer seven "nations" before we ourselves can lay claim to the promised land of heaven. The pagan nations represent the traditional seven deadly sins: pride, anger, gluttony, lust, laziness, envy, and greed.

Captive Audience

There is, according to the early Christians, a second great historical event that symbolizes human sinfulness. It is Judah's captivity in Babylon. Though this exile was much briefer than the enslavement in Egypt, it was no less deadly to the Jewish way of life.

By the sixth century B.C., the chosen people were weakened and divided from many generations of civil strife. The Babylonian king Nebuchadnezzar had little trouble conquering the land of Judah and making it a vassal state to Babylon. He drained the land of its best and brightest citizens, deporting them to his land, to serve his kingdom. There, for seventy years, they served well and were rewarded and respected for their work. Many Jewish men took Babylonian wives. Many tradesmen learned new skills from their Babylonian colleagues. The captive people made great strides, for example, in the science of astronomy, the profession of banking, and the technology of coinage.

The chosen people prospered in the land of their captivity. Perhaps they did too well there, for some began to abandon hope of returning to Judea. They had grown accustomed to Babylonian language, Babylonian streets, Babylonian ways. Again, as in Egypt, they began to slacken in their religious observance and to adopt the ways of their captors. Those who remained faithful to the God of Israel had to struggle mightily, invoking a curse upon themselves if they should grow too comfortable in their captivity:

> *If I forget you, O Jerusalem,*
> *let my right hand wither!*
> *Let my tongue cleave to the roof of my mouth,*
> *if I do not remember you,*
> *if I do not set Jerusalem above my highest joy! (Ps 137:5–6)*

The faithful exile refuses to allow himself even legitimate consolations, for fear that they will ease the pain of his separation from home. He denies himself the joy of singing his favorite songs "by the waters of Babylon" (v. 1).

As Egyptian slavery was a type of original sin, so—for the Church fathers—Babylonian captivity represented actual sin. It's one thing to be born as an Israelite infant in Egypt. It's quite another to be carried off to exile as a direct consequence of your actual sins. Babylon was a captivity brought on by the choice of the captives, and then sustained by their choice. As they grew sated by material comforts in a pagan land, they forgot what it was like to be free in their homeland. Why should they trade their prosperity, security, and comfort for the rough and risky task of resettling and rebuilding Jerusalem?

Why, too, should sinners turn away from fraud—from lying to the IRS—when it's so profitable? Why turn away from gluttony when the finest foods are close at hand? Why turn away from anger when the cleverest putdowns come so readily to mind?

It can be comfortable to remain in sin. But Babylon's comfort comes at a cost: our freedom, our citizenship, our inheritance.

Coming Attractions

"Unfaithful creatures! Do you not know that friendship with the world is enmity with God? Therefore whoever wishes to be a friend of the world makes himself an enemy of God" (Jas 4:4).

We are exiles in the world, and we must never lose sight of that fact. We must never forget who we are, whence we have come, and where we are going. We must live on earth, but we must live *for* heaven.

So, like the chosen people, we must "put to death" the idolatry that remains in us. Like the Babylonian captives, we must deny ourselves not only sinful pleasures, but a certain measure of legitimate pleasures; for these can serve as the bait in the world's trap. It is by our growing attraction and attachment to worldly goods that we turn, by ever greater degrees, away from God.

This is why Jesus taught the apostles to fast. This is why the apostles continued to fast after Jesus ascended to heaven. This is why self-denial has always been a hallmark of true Christianity, made the focus of the forty-day Lenten season every year.

This is also why Jesus could say, in the Beatitudes: "Blessed are you poor . . . Blessed are you that hunger . . . Blessed are you that weep . . . Blessed are you when men hate you, and when they exclude you and revile you, and cast out your name as evil" (Lk 6:20–23). All of these calamities, He said, are cause for rejoicing.

We should not miss the shock value of Jesus' words. Even after twenty centuries of Christian preaching, they are still a radical reversal of worldly values. Like the sacrifice of Egypt's sacred animals, the Beatitudes represent a "normative inversion"; they turn our expectations upside down. We instinctively feel it's a *curse* to be impoverished, hungry, grieving, and slandered. But Jesus presents all these circumstances as moments of blessing. Suffering teaches us detachment from the goods of this world, and so it frees us to attach ourselves to the goods of heaven. This is true of suffering that is actively sought (as in the case of fasting, keeping a vigil, or making a pilgrimage) or suffering passively endured (as in the case of a toothache, a thunderstorm, or a train that's running late). Suffering enables us to say with Saint Paul, "But whatever gain I had, I counted as loss for the sake of Christ. Indeed I count everything as loss because of the surpassing worth of knowing Christ Jesus my Lord. For His sake I have suffered the loss of all things, and count them as refuse [literally, "as dung"], in order that I may gain Christ" (Phil 4:7–8).

All created things are good, simply because God made them. But even the greatest delights—sex, books, chocolate, coffee, wine—are nearer in value to trash or sewage than they are to God!

A Test for the Blessed

As we grow detached from things, we come (with God's help) to master our desires, and we give the mastery over to God. Discipline and divine grace heal the intellect and the will of the effects of concupiscence. We can begin to see things clearly.

And the more clearly we see, the better we can face the daily temptations to turn away from God and toward created things. If we must choose between Christ and dung, there's only one sane and rational choice.

Few people grow so detached as to see matters that way, all the time. Yet that is what God wants from each of us, and He will deny it to no one who asks and is willing to receive the grace, the blessing.

When we face a choice between suffering and sin, we are facing a trial, a test, an ordeal, just as Adam did, just as

the Israelites did in the desert, just as the Jews did in Babylon. If we choose momentary comfort, security, and safety
over eternal love, God will respect our choice. If we choose
momentary suffering for the sake of eternal love, we will
draw nearer to the happiness of the homeland, of heaven.
We will grow more Godlike in the bosom of God Himself.

We are driven by the appetites we have cultivated. We
travel in the direction to which we've turned our bodies, our
hearts, our minds, our eyes. But if we wish to reach our des-
tination—if we wish one day to be home in heaven—we
have to turn away from our earthly attachments and turn directly Godward. It won't do us any good to turn halfway;
that still points us the wrong way. Until we break off our attachments, our conversion will not be complete.

No Bull

Such sacrifice is never easy. Remember, from chapter 2, that
an Israelite making a sin offering had to subdue the animal
victim, bind it, slaughter it, gut it, cut it up, and sing some
hymns. Most of the sacrifices we make won't be so bloody,
but we shouldn't expect them to be any easier. A bull can be
easier to subdue than a body warped by concupiscence.
Then, as now, such sacrifice requires effort, strength, expense, time.

Israel's animal sacrifice was a sign and foreshadowing of
the sacrifice to come. Consequently, when Christ came into
the world, He said, "Sacrifices and offerings You have not

desired, but a body You have prepared for me" (Heb 10:5). We, too, offer the desires of our body, the comforts, and the delights, in sacrifice for our sins, and for the sake of our love for God.

"The sacrifice acceptable to God is a broken spirit, a broken and contrite heart" (Ps 51:17). If we make this minimal beginning, an act of contrition from the heart, God's grace will make up for the rest.

And if you have any doubt where such sacrifice should best begin, just visit the nearest confessional. Conversion is possible without the sacraments, but it's arduous. The grace of the sacraments eases our way.

CHAPTER 10

KNOW PAIN, KNOW GAIN: THE SECRETS OF WINNING PENANCE

I<small>N MOST</small> C<small>HURCH</small> documents, confession is called the sacrament of penance. We use the terms interchangeably to denote the sacrament, but they are not synonymous. *Confession* describes the act of telling one's sin. *Penance* describes two things: an attitude and an action. We spent some of the earlier chapters looking at the meaning of *confession* We'll spend this chapter studying the meaning of penance.

Penance, considered as an attitude, describes the hatred of one's own sins. Penance, in this sense, is a necessary condition for sacramental confession. We have to be sorry for our sins; we have to despise them, to some degree.

Hate Crimes

When our attitude of penance is perfect—when we hate our sins because they have offended God, Whom we love—then we confess our sins with true contrition. Most of the time, though, we have mixed motives for hating our sins. We hate them because we are ashamed of them, or because they make us feel bad, or because we're afraid of being punished, or because they have caused ill effects on our body, mind, finances, or relationships. This imperfect hatred of our sins is called attrition, and it will suffice for a valid confession, though we should always strive for more perfect penance.

When the attitude of penance is habitual, we say that penance is a virtue. This virtue is integral to the Christian life, and it is a grace we should pray for. But we should also work to grow in the virtue of penance by making acts of penance—just as we grow in the virtues of kindness, courage, and industry by repeating many small acts of kindness, courage, and hard work. The virtue of penance, then, becomes a part of our everyday living, a natural and supernatural habitat for the sacrament that shares its name.

Acts of penance, however, are not limited to sacramental confessions. Such acts include any act of self-denial offered to make amends for our sins or the sins of others. In the last chapter, I mentioned fasting, vigils, and pilgrimages; but there are many more. Indeed, the Christian who has the virtue of penance is always eager to make sacrifices for the sake of others, and most of these will be quiet and common actions—the times when we inconvenience ourselves for the sake of another person's comfort, pleasure, or consolation.

Perhaps we suggest going to the movies, because we know that's what our companions would prefer, even though we would really rather go to a ball game.

We deny ourselves a second piece of pie—even though it's the most delicious we've ever tasted—so that someone else might enjoy it instead. Or, on the other hand, we eagerly ask for a second piece of pie—even though it's the worst we've ever tasted—so that a first-time baker's feelings won't be hurt.

We linger for a few minutes with a coworker or neighbor whom we find dull or annoying. Instead of excusing ourselves for a quick exit, we give our time and our close attention.

We complete mundane tasks carefully and promptly, even though we'd rather get a root canal than fill out another five-page form for our employer.

The best acts of penance are those so ordinary that they go unnoticed. Our best days, and our happiest days, are those that are filled with such actions.

Painful Truth

It's important that we get this right, because many people to-day—even some Christians—misunderstand Christian self-denial. They try to dismiss it as psychologically sick, world hating, dour, joyless, and masochistic. No doubt, there are Christians who are psychologically sick, world hating, dour, joyless, and masochistic, but these characteristics are neither the cause nor the effect of Christian self-denial.

The first thing to get straight is that vigorous self-denial is an essential part of the Christian faith. Jesus said, "If any man would come after Me, let him deny himself and take up his cross and follow Me" (Mt 16:24). "Whoever does not bear his own cross and come after Me, cannot be My disciple" (Lk 14:27). Self-denial, clearly, is not optional; there's no alternative, self-indulgent way of salvation available to humankind.

The next thing to clear up is that self-denial is most certainly *not* a denial of the goodness of the world. Christians sacrifice the best of things not because they think the world is evil and must be put to death, but because they know the world is very good—so good that it can distract us from what's far better, thus detouring us on our way home to the Father. Like the Israelites, we may wish to return to Egypt or to dally in Babylon. We may choose to enjoy any number of pleasant pastimes rather than go to confession, go to Mass, or go to visit our grandmother in the nursing home. Again, sin is not a matter of our choosing "evil matter" over "good spirit." It's always a matter of preferring a lesser good instead of a greater good—or instead of goodness itself.

Finally, we must assert that pain is not valuable for its own sake. Christians take no pleasure in pain. We do, however, find blessing in pain, as Christ did.

Idol Talk

Can there be any doubt that the first Christians followed Jesus' admonition to lead a life of penance and self-denial? Consider only Saint Paul, who wrote: "Those who belong to Christ Jesus have crucified the flesh with its passions and desires" (Gal 5:24).

If anyone should wish to impose a purely spiritual or metaphorical reading on that text, Paul gets more specific elsewhere. For example, he willingly accepted the hardships that came his way, from the everyday irritants to the cruelest tortures: "labors, . . . imprisonments, with countless beatings, and often near death. Five times I have received at the hands of the Jews the forty lashes less one. Three times I have been beaten with rods; once I was stoned. Three times I have been shipwrecked; a night and a day I have been adrift at sea; on frequent journeys, in danger from rivers, danger from robbers, danger from my own people, danger from Gentiles, danger in the city, danger in the wilderness, danger at sea, danger from false brethren; in toil and hardship, through many a sleepless night, in hunger and thirst, often without food, in cold and exposure" (2 Cor 11:23–27).

Paul took all of these in a spirit of penance. Yet he did not stop there. He actively undertook other hardships, imposing still more severe discipline on his flesh. "I do not box as one beating the air; but I pommel my body and subdue it, lest after preaching to others I myself should be disqualified" (1 Cor 9:26–27).

Paul did not give in to self-indulgence or the easy life. Quite the contrary: He knew that the body had to be returned to strict control of the mind, the soul, and reason, and that this was no easy task. It required a certain severe determination, which he spoke of in the strongest terms. "If you live according to the flesh you will die, but if by the Spirit you put to death the deeds of the body you will live" (Rom 8:13). *Put to death*— that shocking phrase is a single word in Latin and in earlier English translations of the Scripture. It comes down to *mortification*, which is synonymous with bodily penance.

"Put to death therefore what is earthly in you: fornication, impurity, passion, evil desire, and covetousness, which is idolatry. On account of these the wrath of God is coming" (Col 3:5).

Acts of self-denial—mortification and penance—destroy the obstacles to divine love and our sharing in the divine life. They smash the idols in our life, so that nothing can distract us from loving God.

Dieting Is Not Fast Enough

Think of this is terms of the Israelites' experience. In order to put Egypt behind them, they had to experience the "normative inversion" of sacrificing their captors' sacred animals. The chosen people had to "put to death" the idolatry that had once held them captive.

When we offer acts of penance to God, we practice a similar sort of normative inversion. We "put to death" the desires that captivate our mind. For what is it that arrests our attention and keeps it locked up? Food? Sex? Money? Material possessions—a house, a car, furniture?

Whatever holds us as willing captives is an idol, and it will soon demand sacrifices from us. Idols, too, will demand a "putting to death" because idols, like Yahweh, are jealous gods. Think about our modern idols. For the sake of work, many people eagerly sacrifice their health, their time, their family. For the sake of unbridled sex, many risk their reputation, their health, their marriages, and even their lives. For the sake of gluttonous consumption, many people are willing to trade years of their lives. I won't tire you with statistics, though I could. (Sexually transmitted diseases are epidemic. More than 61 percent of American adults are overweight, and 27 percent of them are obese.)

We all know the captivating power of these idols, the hold they have on our lives. We all know the sacrifices they will eventually demand from us; the surgeon general tells us so, with some regularity. Moreover, we're even willing to recognize that we need to do something about these idols—put them to death. There are few truths as self-evident as the old Christian adage: The body wants more than it needs, so we must give it less than it wants. We know we need to diet. We need to spend less time at work and more at home. We need to be less preoccupied with sex. And so on. But these natural solutions are not enough. For there's an absurd human tendency to idolize the natural instrument that destroys our idols. The ex-drinker, ex-smoker, ex–chubby person, ex-philanderer too often becomes an obnoxious and fanatical devotee of the fad diet or the twelve-step program that "saved" him.

We mustn't fall into that trap. That's why we need to supernaturalize our self-denial—make it penance—offer it to God, the one true God, the only God Who saves. Idols must be replaced by a pure and divine devotion, and our devotion must be purified by our attitude of penance and our acts of penance.

The Big Picture

Context is key here. If we don't see the big picture, sacrifice will make no sense to us, or it will make a perverted sort of sense.

The context of our sacrifice is a relationship, a personal relationship, a love relationship, a family relationship, a covenant relationship.

It is not odd for family members to make sacrifices for the sake of one another. A parent's life is fairly defined by such sacrifices. A dad "puts to death" the things that keep him from loving his children as he should. A mom "puts to death" her peeves, her comforts, her cravings, so that she can be free to raise children who are happy, wise, and strong. A child, over time, learns to subdue bodily cravings and impulses for the sake of a healthy family life (potty training, regular sleep habits, no eating between meals). The child, in turn, grows into an adult, a caregiver, who must give time and attention to Mom and Dad, as age and illness take their toll.

Love requires that we make sacrifices for the sake of our beloved. A man who is smitten with a woman doesn't think twice about staying up late to write her a love poem. He doesn't hesitate to offer her his gloves on a bitter winter day, even if his own hands are nearly frozen. If she says she dislikes his sweater or his cologne, he moves the offending matter to the back of the closet or the bottom of the trash can. A man in love will redouble his heroic efforts if he has somehow offended his beloved. He wants to make up posthaste, with not a minute to spare for delay.

All of these are natural acts of self-denial that people offer spontaneously for the sake of love. For those who are in love, sacrifice comes more easily, and even the pains endured are thought of as being sweet. There is no questioning the necessity of detachment from anything that presents an obstacle to the relationship.

Thus, we see that sacrifice, self-denial, penance, and mortification are hardly odd or unusual activities in the natural order. We are willing to sacrifice for goals we can see. We must learn to sacrifice for the sake of a love unseen, putting to death the sin, temptation, and the disorder of concupiscence, all of which render us likely to offend our Beloved.

On Earth as in Heaven

Sacrifice, however, is not merely negative. It is not just a "killing." It is also a giving. Our small sacrifices are symbolic of the total self-giving that is essential to love. People in love give themselves entirely.

Indeed, the Church teaches that human love shows us the "certain likeness between the union of the divine Persons" and humanity, which is made in the divine image. When we give ourselves in love, we imitate God. For "God is love" (1 Jn 4:16), and the essence of love is life-giving.

Consider the inner life of the Trinity. The Father pours out the fullness of Himself; He holds nothing of His divinity back. He gives all His life. He eternally fathers the Son. The Father is, above all else, a life-giving lover, and the Son is His perfect image. So what else is the Son but a life-giving lover? And the Son dynamically images the Father for all eternity, pouring out the life He's received from the Father; He gives that life back to the Father as a perfect expression of thanks and love. That life and love, which the Son receives from the Father and returns to the Father, *is* the Holy Spirit.

When God became man in Jesus Christ, His life on earth was an image in time of the divine life in eternity. Jesus' life was a complete gift of Himself, given over the course of thirty-some years. Everything within His life—His forgiveness, healing, teaching, preaching—was an incarnation of the transcendent love that abides eternally.

The love that is God is the only love that can satisfy us and make us happy. Our human loves themselves will fail us, through human weakness, imperfection, or death. Human loves—and the limited happiness they bring—are just a hint of the love for which God created us. We will not be happy, we will not know love, until we love like God, until we love *as gods* (Ps 82:6; see also Jn 10:34), partakers in the divine nature (2 Pet 1:4). Man, says the Church, "is the only creature on earth which God willed for itself, [and] cannot fully find himself except through a sincere gift of himself."

If we understand penance in this context, it makes sense. For we cannot imagine love without sacrifice. We cannot truly love *this* person unless we "put to death" *that* vice, that obstacle, that peeve or preference.

This is why the ancient covenants required sacrifice. The covenants created a family bond, and the sacrifice was symbolic of the former bonds that were now severed, now put to death. The covenant was also symbolic of the total self-gift, without which love and family life are impossible.

Removing Obstacles to God's Love

Penance becomes warped—psychologically sick, world hating, dour, joyless, or masochistic—only when it is practiced or considered apart from love, in which case, anyway, it is not true penance.

Keep in mind what penance is not, and you'll always be clear about what penance is. It's not suffering for the sake of suffering. It's not the gross imposition of a sadistic God or an authoritarian Church.

Penance is, rather, the willing removal of any obstacles to God's love for us and our love of God. It is an inchoate giving of our whole self, moment by moment, to God.

Our gift of self, unlike God's, is gradual, given over a lifetime. By nature and by God's grace, each act of penance we offer, each sacramental confession, every little sacrifice conforms us ever more to God's image, makes our lives more resemble the divine life. We accomplish this, partly, through the natural methods of self-mastery, but overwhelmingly through our correspondence to God's grace.

Acts of self-denial have a medicinal effect on our concupiscence. They heal us by offsetting our many acts of self-indulgence. They serve as a remedy for the acts of self-indulgence by which we've sinned or weakened our will.

The small penance we receive in the confessional works the same way. However, it works more effectively than days of fasting, because it packs the additional power of Christ's sacramental grace. Sacramental penance must not be our only act of penance, but it will always be our surest, because it was instituted by Christ for that purpose.

The sacrament of penance is an act of penance best practiced with an attitude of penance within the context of a life of penance.

CHAPTER 11

THINKING OUTSIDE THE BOX: HABITS OF HIGHLY EFFECTIVE PENITENTS

I F PENANCE IS a way of life, how—in the everyday, nitty-gritty details—are we supposed to live the sacrament of penance?

The sacrament is the high point of such a life. It's the culmination of all our penitential acts of sacrifice, and it surpasses them all by several orders of magnitude, because the sacrament is the means given by providence to restore and renew the covenantal bond of our supernatural life with God. The sacrament has been instituted by Christ to give grace. It is an act of God—this sacramental forgiveness of sins—on a par with the creation of the world. Moreover, unlike our other voluntary penances, the sacrament produces its effects by the power of Christ alone, and not at all by our own labors or the labors of our priest-confessor. The Latin theological term for this is *ex opere operato*, which means "by the very fact of the actions being performed" (see *CCC* 1128).

If we are to live a life that is true to the biblical worldview, we cannot and must not live without frequent confession that is carefully prepared and fully integrated into our habits of prayer.

When I Am Weekly, Then I Am Strong

The Church insists that we go to confession at least once a year, to confess any serious sins of the year gone by. This used to be called the Easter Duty, as many Catholics fulfilled it in time to make a good Communion during the Easter season.

But if you study the lives of the saints, you'll see that more frequent confession is the norm, monthly the minimum. I am one of the growing number of Catholics who try to get to the sacrament once a week. Less than a century ago, weekly confession was the normal practice in many parishes, when Catholics young and old stood in long lines every Saturday to await their brief moment in the box. I'm not sure what happened to reverse this trend, but I feel certain it wasn't a decline in the number or seriousness of sins committed by American Catholics.

There are many good reasons for making a confession every week or every month.

First of all, it's easier than going once a year. That may sound strange, but it's true. The more we go to confession, the better we become at it. Like my tennis serve, it gets easier and smoother with practice.

It's easier also because we're dealing with a shorter span of time. If the just man falls seven times a day, that means the most virtuous folks in town, if they're confessing once a year, have at least 2,555 sins to sort through (2,562 during leap year). A week's span, or even a month, is far more manageable and allows for a more sincere and complete confession.

More frequent confession means a more effective program of growth in virtue and a more thorough conquest of habitual sins. Let's face it: Spiritual growth, like physical conditioning, doesn't come easy. We'd all like to shed our sinful habits overnight, just as I'd be pleased to drop twenty pounds by tomorrow morning or triple my muscular strength by next week. But changes in character are, like changes in our bodies, rarely discernible from week to week or month to month. Only over the course of years or decades do we notice a difference. We need to have a regimen, and we need to stick with it over the long haul.

People often get frustrated because they seem to rehash the same sins every time they confess. Yes, that can be humiliating, but it could be much worse. It would be worse, for example, for us to commit new sins! If we don't seem to be getting better, at least we can see that we're not getting worse—which is what would likely happen if we stopped going to confession. Making the same confession over and over is humiliating—I don't deny that—but humiliation isn't such a bad thing for a Christian; it is, after all, the thing that makes us humble. Humility, then, takes out sin at its source, which is pride. All this is to the good, for God finds humility irresistible, and He opposes the proud—even when they're right.

We need to stay with the sacrament for the long haul, even though we sometimes feel frustrated. Most people, over time, notice that they're not confessing *all* the same sins as they committed ten years ago. As we make progress in one area, through grace and through effort, we notice other areas that need work. We can move onward, upward, and Godward, if we persevere.

The last, but not the least, reason for frequent confession is Saint Paul's warning to the Christians of Corinth: "Whoever, therefore, eats the bread or drinks the cup of the Lord in an unworthy manner will be guilty of profaning the body and blood of the Lord. . . . That is why many of you are weak and ill, and some have died" (1 Cor 11:27, 30). If we say we are without sins, we're liars. If we sin but don't confess, we're inhospitable to Jesus, Whom we receive in Communion. If we're welcoming a divine guest into our hearts on Sunday, we should at least do spiritual housecleaning on Saturday. Think of how we would clean our homes if we were inviting a date, a dignitary, or our boss over for dinner.

Jesus Himself told a parable of a rich man who, out of mercy, invited many unworthy people to his son's wedding feast (Mt 22:1–14). Both "bad and good" people attended, but only one was cast out, and that was the man who showed up without a wedding garment. The meaning of the parable could not be clearer: God the Father, through His mercy, invites us all to the Eucharist, which is the marriage supper of His Son and the Church (see also Rev 19:9, 21:9–10). We must, however, take care to prepare ourselves properly for the occasion. To do otherwise would be a sign of ingratitude and presumption. Jesus is no less severe than Saint Paul in describing the consequences: "Then the king said to the attendants: 'Bind him hand and foot, and cast him into the outer darkness; there men will weep and gnash their teeth.' "

Finding a Confessor

Our confession should be not only frequent, but programmatic. We should have goals for overcoming sin and growing in virtue, and we should be working toward the achievement of those goals. We can do this much more easily if we establish an ongoing relationship with a confessor.

A confessor who comes to know us will come to know, better than we do, the obstacles between us and heaven. A regular confessor will know our circumstances in life, our peculiar temptations, our strengths, and our weaknesses. Thus equipped, he can watch for patterns. He can trace our sins back to a dominant fault. And he can advise us on the best ways to move forward. Also, he can pray specifically for our struggles, and we should never underestimate the value of that. A regular confessor can be like a family physician, who comes to know us over time, to know our habits, know our living and working conditions, and know what really ails us.

Finding the right confessor might require time and effort. You'll need to ask around and maybe visit many confessionals before you land in the right one—which might not be the one that makes you feel good. There are people who go from confessional to confessional until they find a priest who will tell them that their sins aren't really sins. But, as a friend of mine put it, if we do this, we're not really looking for a new confessor; we're looking for a new god, one who will come around to our way of thinking about morality. That's consumerism at its most deadly. It's like shopping around till we find a doctor who will lie to us about the results of a blood test. It might leave us feeling relieved for a while, but in the end it will kill us." Amen to that. And what will kill those who shop for a new god is the self-inflicted spiritual death of mortal sin.

There is much debate about whether it is best to ask one's confessor for more intensive spiritual direction as well, or whether we should seek a separate spiritual director for the detail work. This book is not the place to examine the issue. I will offer only two observations. (1) Ongoing guidance is indispensable to ongoing growth. The old adage is true: The man who has himself for a lawyer has a fool for a client. You and I *need* to have a spiritual director. (2) If finding a willing, faithful confessor proves extremely difficult, we might not have the luxury of hunting for a second willing, faithful priest to be our spiritual director.

Get Ready, Get Set . . .

If we've found a confessional, found a time, found a priest, we still have some preparation to do. We need to search out the sins we've committed so that we can make a confession that's complete and contrite.

The habit that helps us to do this is called examination of conscience. This is a periodic review of our thoughts, words, deeds, and omissions. It's a searching of our memory in order to uncover our sins and detect any patterns in our temptations or behavior. The exam makes us aware of our progress, or regress, and keeps us focused on what's real. Without this honest scrutiny, we can make countless excuses for ourselves and for our sins and infidelities to God and neighbor. Or we can avert our eyes again and again, choosing to look at anything rather than our own lives.

We should try to make our exam at least daily. Like a vitamin, an exercise regimen, a diet, or bookkeeping, it won't work well until we're faithful to it every day. Many spiritual writers prescribe bedtime as the best time, because the day is all behind us then. Pope John XXIII, however, recommended a second exam, at midday, so that we can correct our course while there is still plenty of day ahead of us. We might take brief notes at each exam, to mark our concerns, struggles, and sins (in a private code). These notes will prove very helpful as we prepare for confession.

There are many good methods for making an examination of conscience. The simplest way is to take a chronological look at the day, from waking till the moment of examination. Another popular way is to consider each of the Ten Commandments and to determine how well you lived them today. Some prayer books give a series of questions for self-examination. (I offer examples in Appendix C, at the end of this book.) Some people like to compile their own list of questions, based on their past experience of weakness or on the suggestions or complaints they receive from coworkers, friends, and family members.

Our nightly examination should be brief, just five minutes or so, ending with an act of contrition. But, to prepare for confession, we should plan to spend more time in prayerful consideration of our sins.

Tradition tells us that the examination of conscience should actually be divided into two: the general exam and the particular exam. The general exam is the one I have just described: a run-through of all the day's events. The particular exam focuses instead on how well we are practicing a particular virtue or avoiding a particular sin. Some people place the particular exam at midday and the general exam at night.

What are the best time, place, and method for the exams? Only you can answer that question for yourself (though, of course, with help from your spiritual director). Experiment to see what works. The important thing is to do it.

If we prepare ourselves well for confession, we will truly get more out of confession. The sacraments confer their grace *ex opere operato*, but what we do with that grace is our business. Sacraments are not magical spells, and God does not sanctify us without our cooperation. Christ gives freely, but we receive only what we are ready, willing, and able to receive. Our good preparation opens our souls to receive more of the grace that Christ is giving us.

And . . . Go!

The most effective habit of highly effective penitents is the habit of confession itself. They do it; they do it often; they do it as well as they can. The great American convert

Dorothy Day described it well from the penitent's side of the screen.

> Going to confession is hard—hard when you have sins to confess, hard when you haven't, and you rack your brain for even the beginnings of sins against charity, chastity, sins of detraction, sloth, or gluttony. You do not want to make too much of your constant imperfections and venial sins, but you want to drag them out to the light of day as the first step in getting rid of them. The just man falls seven times daily.
>
> "Bless me, Father, for I have sinned," is the way you begin. "I made my last confession a week ago, and since then . . ."
>
> "I have sinned. These are my sins." That is all you are supposed to tell; not the sins of others, or your own virtues, but only your ugly, gray, drab, monotonous sins.

It's not very glamorous or romantic. It's work, and as such it involves some sweat of the brow. But, even in the natural order, work is what puts food on the table and gives us a sense of accomplishment; work is what enables us to move forward, to get ahead in life. In the supernatural order, "we are God's coworkers" (1 Cor 3:9) in the work of our own salvation. The work of confession is what wins us the grace to get ahead in the spiritual life; and it puts food on the Eucharistic table for us.

From the confessor's side of the screen, Saint Josemaría Escrivá, a priest of the twentieth century, gave the best advice I've seen for what to do once we're in the confessional. He counseled his penitents to follow the four C's. Make your confession complete, contrite, clear, and concise.

Make it complete. Don't omit any mortal sins, of course, but make sure to include the venial sins that are giving you trouble. Most importantly, don't drop the sins that embarrass you. It's best to start your confession with the sin that's toughest to admit. After that, it can only get easier.

Make it contrite. Be sorry for your sins. Remember that it is God you have offended, and He has loved you lavishly and unstintingly.

Make it clear. Don't be subtle. Don't cover over your sins with euphemisms. Make sure the priest understands what you mean.

But make it concise. There's no need to go into gory detail. Often when we do, we're just trying to excuse ourselves by inventing special circumstances or blaming others. Besides, the priest's time is valuable and will be well spent with another penitent.

Again, though, the important thing is to make it! Don't put it off till another day.

CHAPTER 12

THE HOME FRONT:
CONFESSION AS COMBAT

T HE ATTITUDE OF penance, the practice of penance, the habits of penance, the sacrament of penance: All of these serve as reminders of who we are. We are children of a loving Father, a lavishly wealthy Father; but we are living far from home, in shameful conditions. Our daily examination of conscience and our weekly or monthly confession will help us to keep our story straight—and to make straight our way homeward.

Still, the homeward journey will be demanding. For our holy nation is a nation at war, and our unholy enemies ever surround us.

Life During Wartime

Serious Christians have always seen life as a battle. This is the dominant metaphor from Saint Augustine's *Christian Combat* to the song "Onward, Christian Soldiers." And it's no less relevant in our own day. The only way Adam's descendants can overcome temptation is through all-out warfare on the things that keep us from God.

In any battle, there are multiple enemies: some seen and some unseen. In addition to struggling against enemy snipers, combatants struggle against discouragement, fatigue, self-doubt. The spiritual combat is no different. Our struggle is against the world, the flesh, and the devil. We are weakened by fleshly concupiscence, and so we find the world and its delights more attractive than God. The devil knows our vulnerability and concentrates his efforts wherever he can weaken us further. When we fail, we may grow sad and tired, and then the devil has achieved a great victory: We have become our own worst enemy.

A soldier who lacks discipline is not up to this fight. This is why Catholics willingly undergo spiritual exercises. We need to be strong in order to overcome formidable temptations. For we know many examples of great people who failed, from Adam to Saint Peter.

Indeed, the odds against us seem so overwhelming that we can be tempted to give up the fight before firing a shot. But we must never let our defenses down. We should instead redouble our efforts, moving the battle further from the city walls, avoiding even the circumstances that would tempt us, avoiding every occasion of sin.

In the case of temptations to mortal sin, we must flee without looking back, just as Lot fled from Sodom (see Gen 19:15–23). There is sin so bad that it mustn't be fought in direct engagement. When we feel passionately prone to grave sin—a sexual sin, for example—we must remove ourselves immediately from the circumstances that tempt us. It is no shame for a weakened soldier to beat retreat from a deadly and far superior foe. If he preserves his life, he will live to fight again. Discretion is the better part of valor.

Mystical Bodies

Whether we succeed or fail, we never fight alone. The "great cloud of witnesses" that surround us (Heb 12:1) are not passive bystanders. They are allies in the battle. Those who are saints in heaven have won victory for us by their own merits. If we call upon them for help, God will credit their righteousness to our cause. Since the Protestant Reformation, Christians have been divided on this notion of the "treasury of merits"; but the biblical concept is actually older than the New Testament. Rabbi Nahum Sarna, echoing the ancient rabbis, wrote in his commentary on Genesis: "God delivered Lot from the catastrophe through the merit of Abraham. This 'doctrine of merit' is a not infrequent theme in the Bible and constitutes the first of many incidents in which the righteousness of chosen individuals may sustain other individuals or even an entire group through its protective power." Rabbi Sarna finds further evidence of the doctrine from the lives of Moses, Samuel, Amos, Jeremiah, and Ezekiel.

To that impressive roster I would add the name of Job, who was not even an Israelite. Still, he was a righteous man; and, living only by the light of the natural law, he knew that he could extend the merits of his life and his sacrifices for the benefit of his sons and daughters: The Bible tells us that Job "would rise early in the morning and offer burnt offerings according to the number of [his children]; for Job said, 'It may be that my sons have sinned, and cursed God in their hearts' " (Jb 1:5).

If the children of a virtuous pagan could draw from their father's merits, how much more can we, who follow in a long line of Christian saints? The treasury of merit has not been depleted. We, too, may draw from this war chest. But we must also contribute to it. We must offer our efforts not only for our own sake, but for the sake of others, our friends, neighbors, family members, and even people we don't know, because they are our cocombatants. Just as the merits of the saints work to our advantage, so our penances will work to the advantage of others. Saint Paul said: "Now I rejoice in my sufferings for your sake, and in my flesh I complete what is lacking in Christ's afflictions for the sake of His body, that is, the Church" (Col 1:24).

The Church is the body of Christ (1 Cor 12:27; Eph 4:12), and we are individually His members (Rom 12:4–5; 1 Cor 6:15, 12:12). Whenever we choose to do good, we build up our fellow fighters, because there is a mystical solidarity that unites us.

On the other hand, when we choose to do evil, we do not sin in isolation, but we weaken our side in the battle. We aid and abet our enemies instead: the devil's network of allies in this world.

This solidarity among combatants is real. Every time we sin, we diminish not only ourselves, but also the Church. That is one reason why Christ has us confess our sins to the Church.

The mystical body of Christ, the communion of saints, finds its strength in the sacrament of penance. One of the great literary critics of the twentieth century, Wallace Fowlie, recognized this immediately when he, then a Protestant, wandered into a poor French-American parish church in New England.

> Half of the penitents, on their knees, were praying, and the others were looking into space. A child left the confessional box and another took his place. In a few seconds the boy had reached the front of the church and knelt at the altar rail. I wondered what sins he had just whispered and what new purity filled him. . . . *I was in a strange house which permitted me a union with many lives, with many millions of lives.* The child at the altar rail was clutching in his left hand a dark blue ski cap, and his heart was speaking to eternity. This penitence in a church I had never known. I had never waited in line for Him, and I had never heard Him speak in a little half-minute accorded by some human sense of justice.

This moment and its realization proved a turning point for Fowlie, who entered the Catholic Church shortly thereafter. Our "strange house" became his own home—became *his* Father's house.

Logs and Specks

We live in a family home that permits us "union with many lives, with many millions of lives." So many people depend upon us: the saints in heaven, our contemporaries on earth, and the future generations who must draw, one day, from our merits.

So we must hate all sin with a holy hatred, but especially our own sins. It's too easy to hate the sins of others—the big sins that are blatantly evil, like genocide or racism, or the intentional sins that hurt us personally, like slights and insults. But the sins that should really matter to us are the sins we commit ourselves. Jesus said: "Why do you see the speck that is in your brother's eye, but do not notice the log that is in your own eye?" (Mt 7:3). The most important and hateful sins in my life are my own. My sins hurt me far more than the sins of all my coworkers, neighbors, and family members combined.

Our love of God is nothing—it's just sentimental simpering—unless it's accompanied by a passionate hatred of our own sins. Want to measure how much you love the Lord? Ask yourself (as I do): Am I more upset by church scandals or political malfeasance than I am with the sins I have committed this week? Am I more conscious of my boss's injustices—or my coworkers', or my spouse's, or my children's injustices—than I am of my own? When we are honest with ourselves, these questions are most painful.

We must oppose all sin, beginning with our own, as a father opposes intruders in his home. We have so much at stake. There is no sin too small to merit our contempt. Saint

Augustine warns us: "A man, so long as he bears the flesh, cannot but have some light sins. But these that we call light, do not make light of. . . . Many light make one huge sin; many drops fill the river; many grains make the lump. And what hope is there? Before all, confession!"

Confession is our hope before everything else! Now, there's an ancient testimony from a sinner who persevered and won the war for his repentance.

The Odds Are God's

When the odds are against us and the battle seems lost, we need never give up hope, because confession can accomplish in us what we cannot, and God's grace in the sacrament is stronger than anything the devil can work against us. God's power to save, heal, and create anew is infinitely stronger than our power to sin and to destroy. "I have swept away your transgressions like a cloud, and your sins like mist; return to me, for I have redeemed you" (Is 44:22). Jesus is the Lamb of God Who "takes away the sin of the world" (Jn 1:29). He *takes sin away*, at its source. He doesn't just forgive sin; He uproots it by removing our sinful heart. But then He goes one better still. He creates in you and me a new heart, a clean heart, as if we hadn't soiled the first one He gave us. "A new heart I will give you, and a new spirit I will put within you; and I will take out of your flesh the heart of stone and give you a heart of flesh" (Ezek 36:26).

Christ is invincible. We, too, will be, if only we return to fight by His side.

With friends like Jesus and His saints, who heeds enemies?

We are prodigal children in a far country. For our own good, we need to get home. But first we must desire it, and then we must make the long, hard journey to get there.

At every stage we must depend on the clear sight we gain through sacramental confession. For it does us no good to fool ourselves or others about our condition. We cannot wish away our sins; and all the New Age visualization techniques we can try won't change our pigsty into a hot tub, the pigs into Shetland ponies, or the hog fodder into lobster tail.

There is no real alternative to repentance. If we don't repent, we'll resent; and if we don't confess, we'll project our guilt onto others. We'll blame our victims. We'll blame our parents. We'll blame the government. We'll blame the boss or the board of directors. We'll blame our heredity. We'll blame our environment. But all this is a distraction. Who are we really blaming? There is only one Lord over heredity and environment. If we don't confess our sins, we, like Adam, will end by blaming God.

Your Heart's Desire

If we do not confess our sins—if we do not live a life of penance—we will always feel that life is a losing battle. We will never get our story straight, because the narrative will be obscured by our excuses and blame-throwing. We will never have anything resembling a biblical worldview, and so we will never see the world as it really is, but only as the dark passage it became for Adam and Cain, or the feeding trough it became for the wayward and worldly Israelites.

We spend much of our prayer life listing off our desires to God. This isn't a bad thing, but penance leads us to a better way. Through our acts of penance, God changes our desires so that we no longer want what we crave, but what we really *need* to gain eternity, to share in the divine nature.

Your acts of penance will win for you the new heart you need. And sacramental confession blesses, completes, and magnifies the power of your everyday penance, so that—in the word's of the ritual's final prayer—"whatever good you do and suffering you endure [may] heal your sins, help you to grow in holiness, and reward you with eternal life.

"Go in peace."

CHAPTER 13

THE OPEN DOOR

I F JESUS HADN'T left us the sacrament of confession, we'd probably have to invent it. For God made us with a need that only confession can fulfill.

Those who know the consolation of confessing their sins tend to cling to it tenaciously. The Protestant reformer Martin Luther wanted to dispense with all the sacraments but baptism and Eucharist; but his instincts prevailed upon him, and he "added the sacrament of penance to these two." He explained why: "Without doubt, confession of sins is necessary, and in accordance with the divine commandments. . . . As for secret confession as practiced today, . . . it seems a highly satisfactory practice to me; it is useful and even necessary. I would not wish it to cease; rather I rejoice that it exists in the church of Christ, for it is a singular medicine for afflicted consciences." Even today, the *Lutheran Book of Worship* includes a rite for auricular confession.

Those who discover confession as adults find it irresistible. The Protestant apologist C. S. Lewis felt the attraction, but had to overcome a deep-seated prejudice against any practices that had the "whiff of Rome" about them. In 1940, he resolved to take up the practice, but he admitted that "the decision was the hardest I have ever made." He confessed regularly, afterward, to an Anglican monk.

Luther clung to confession even as he left the Catholic Church. Lewis sought it outside the Catholic Church.

There are Protestants, however, who neither knew the Church's practice as children nor encountered it in a positive way as adults—and yet even they find themselves reinventing the penitential wheel, one spoke at a time.

Unpaid Bills

In 1979, I found myself a first-year divinity student at a prestigious evangelical Protestant seminary. My wife, Kimberly, and I were newly wed, and both of us looked forward to a lifetime of service in the Presbyterian ministry.

I relished my prospects. I loved my studies. I felt strong in my faith.

But something kept gnawing at my conscience. It was the unpaid bills of my delinquent teen years. How many hundreds of dollars' worth of record albums had I stolen before my conversion to Christianity? The question gnawed at me. I read Exodus 22, the chapter that mandates twofold and fourfold restitution for acts of theft, and I was cut to the heart—convicted (see Ex 22:1 and Lk 19:1–10).

I felt I was a hypocrite—studying theology, witnessing to the Gospel, preparing for ministry, when I had never made matters right with those I had wronged. Sure, I had confessed my sin to God in my heart and I had apologized to my parents, but I knew there was something more to be done.

After much prayer, I took up the matter with Kimberly. Though we had hardly any money, she agreed that I was duty-bound to make fourfold restitution to the stores I had victimized.

I racked my memory, trying to recall each instance of shoplifting, where it had occurred and how much I had stolen. I came up with fairly accurate estimates and the names of several establishments. Then I took a deep breath and started calling.

The responses I received were varied and curious. A couple of the places actually could not accommodate me, except by listening to my apology. Their accounting practices gave them no category for accepting long-deferred payment for long-lost merchandise. An employee at one store, however, was well prepared for my offer. He told me that the store had received many such offers by "born-again Christians" and so had set up a "restitution fund."

I made my most valiant effort; and I gladly paid the last cent of my savings. Christmas was coming, and Kimberly and I had no money to buy gifts. But we didn't care. We made personal, craftsy gifts out of scraps we had at hand; yet many of our family members told us they were the best presents that they had received, and they still cherish them today.

For the first time in years, I felt completely clean, light as a feather, peaceful as heaven itself.

I didn't know it at the time, but the joy I knew was the

joy of confessing my sins, doing penance, and making satisfaction.

Restitution can be liberating, and it is sometimes necessary (see *CCC*, n. 2412). The Church does not, however, hold us strictly to the Mosaic laws in this matter. Not everyone is required to apologize personally for every sin of their past life. Indeed, in the case of some sins (sexual sins, for example), it could be spiritually disastrous to attempt any kind of personal contact or restitution.

What the Church does is give us a time and a place where we can unburden our souls and receive the counsel and the grace we need to make things right.

Bring It on Home

Our experience of mercy in the confessional cannot help but spill over into our everyday lives. Remember the words of Jesus: "Be merciful, even as your Father is merciful" (Lk 6:36). In fact, Jesus was insistent on this point, teaching that the measure of mercy we receive depends on the mercy we dispense to others. "For with the judgment you pronounce you will be judged, and the measure you give will be the measure you get" (Mt 7:2). Saint James writes a chilling conclusion: "For judgment is without mercy to one who has shown no mercy" (Jas 2:13).

God established a way for us to seek and receive mercy. It is a sacramental way: spiritual yet material, both heavenly and earthly. We, too, must find ways—concrete, specific ways—to bring mercy to our homes, our workplaces, and our neighborhoods. For we cannot keep God's mercy for ourselves unless we also give it away to others.

There is an infinite variety of ways we might do this, imitating the love of God in the unique particulars of our lives. In my family, we've adopted the custom of the "day of jubilee." It's an old idea, really. As a matter of fact, it's an *Old Testament* idea. In ancient Israel, a "jubilee year" was supposed to occur every fiftieth year (see Lev 25:8–55). During that year, debts were forgiven, slaves set free, and all people returned to the lands of their inheritance. It was a time of family restoration and of reconciliation between the generations.

All of which appeals to me when I feel like something's wrong in our home. If I can't get the children to come forward to confess to a problem, I sometimes announce a family jubilee, a time when anyone might come forward to confess a fault or wrongdoing without fear of punishment.

I have been continually amazed by the changes this custom has worked in our home life and in the lives of individual children. In some cases, it has been the occasion for tremendous personal breakthroughs. The lesson it brings home—the lesson I learn every time I go to confession—is that what matters most is right relationships and not just doing everything according to the rules.

God has been lavishly merciful with us. In the Old Covenant, the jubilee came every half-century. You were lucky if you lived to see one. Even Passover came only once a year. In the New Covenant, however, the jubilee comes as often as we wish to receive the sacrament.

God's mercy is lavish. It is not merely a suspension of justice; it's a paternal patience in helping us to achieve justice, at a slow pace, because we're His children. Knowing how God works mercy in His family, we should eagerly strive to replicate His mercy in our own families.

Saint Leo the Great said: "Mercy wishes that you be merciful. Justice wants you to be just, so the Creator wishes to see Himself reflected in His creature, and God wishes His image to be reproduced in the mirror of the human heart."

Low Frequency

I began this book—I must confess—with some degree of fear and trembling. The sacrament of reconciliation has fallen into disuse in the country in which I live. Some parishes have pulled back to a half-hour per week of posted times for confession. Others have pulled all the way back and now offer the sacrament only by appointment. The pastors say there's little demand. And they're probably not surprised. A recent study concluded that almost half of our priests avail *themselves* of the sacrament only "once or twice a year," "rarely," or "never."

Yet never has the world known such need for the sacrament. We can't live without it, though we continually try by looking for substitutes. Some people seek escape from their sins through drugs or codependent relationships; others seek relief through counseling or other therapies. While all of these might help us mask the symptoms, none, ultimately, can cure the disease. Only by confessing our sins do we allow the Lamb of God to take them away.

We need confession. The longing for mercy that has consumed countless canonized saints—not to mention Martin Luther and C. S. Lewis—has not diminished in the least. Indeed, it has grown stronger. For we live in anxious times, when many people feel locked out of the family home—the home of their Father God. And for those who want to get back to the hearth and the table, confession is the key. Better still, the confessional is the open doorway to the only home that will ever satisfy us.

Jesus Himself said, "I am the door; if anyone enters by Me, he will be saved" (Jn 10:9). It's a simple statement, but it implies a lot of mercy, for we are all sinners, and even the best of us (says the Bible) fall seven times a day!

The Healing Power of Mercy

Jesus is infinite mercy, and He shares His mercy infinitely through His Church, in the sacrament of confession. Confession is key to our spiritual growth, and it is the ordinary way that we believers come to a deeper knowledge of ourselves as we truly are—that is, as God sees us. Confession keeps us from living and laboring under delusions about the world, about our place in it, and about the story of our lives. It brings the dark corners of our soul into the clear morning light of eternal day, for ourselves to see in the sight of God. That can be difficult, and it can sometimes be painful, but in the end it heals with the all-powerful touch of Jesus Christ.

Through confession, we begin to heal. We begin to get

our stories straight. We come home through the open door, to resume our place in God's family. We begin to know peace.

Again, none of this comes easily. Indeed, confession doesn't make change easy, but it does make it possible, supernatural, and salvific—not just for ourselves, but for every life we touch. Confession is not a quick fix, but it is a sure cure. We need to go to the sacrament, and go again, and keep going back, because life is a marathon, not a forty-yard dash. We'll often want to stop, but like a distance runner, we need to press on for our second wind, and our third, and our fourth. In this case, we can count on the wind coming, because it's the "wind" of the Holy Spirit.

When I speak of the continual need for confession, I speak with authority. I am an inveterate sinner, though one who has found his way, again and again, to kneel and be healed at the throne of God's mercy.

APPENDICES

I'm closing this book with a prayer for my readers—and a treasury of prayers and guides. In the following appendices, you'll find resources that have proven helpful to me, my family, and my friends through the years. I pray they will help you, too.

APPENDIX A:
RITE FOR RECONCILIATION
OF INDIVIDUAL PENITENTS

RECEPTION OF THE PENITENT

When the penitent comes to confess his sins, the priest welcomes him warmly and greets him with kindness.

Then the penitent makes the sign of the cross, which the priest may make also:

In the name of the Father, and of the Son, and of the Holy Spirit. Amen.

The priest invites the penitent to have trust in God, in these or similar words:

May God, Who has enlightened every heart,
help you to know your sins and trust in His mercy.

The penitent answers: **Amen.**

READING OF THE WORD OF GOD (OPTIONAL)

Then the priest may read or say from memory a text of Scripture that proclaims God's mercy and calls man to conversion.

CONFESSION OF SINS AND ACCEPTANCE OF SATISFACTION

Where it is the custom, the penitent says a general formula of confession (for example, **"I confess to almighty God . . ."**) before he confesses his sins. If necessary, the priest helps the penitent to make an integral confession and gives him suitable counsel. He urges him to be sorry for his faults, reminding him that through the sacrament of penance the Christian dies and rises with Christ and is thus renewed in the paschal mystery. The priest proposes an act of penance, which the penitent accepts in order to make satisfaction for sin and to amend his life. The priest should make sure that he adapts his counsel to the penitent's circumstances.

PRAYER OF THE PENITENT AND ABSOLUTION

The priest then asks the penitent to express his sorrow, which the penitent may do in these or similar words:

> My God, I am sorry for my sins with all my heart. In choosing to do wrong and failing to do good, I have sinned against You, Whom I should love above all things. I firmly intend, with Your help, to do penance, to sin no more, and to avoid whatever leads me to sin. Our Savior Jesus Christ suffered and died for us. In His name, my God, have mercy.

Other prayers of the penitent may be chosen, such as:

> *Lord Jesus, Son of God,*
> *have mercy on me, a sinner.*

Then the priest extends his hands over the penitent's head (or at least extends his right hand) and says:

> God the Father of mercies, through the death and resurrection of His Son has reconciled the world to Himself and sent the Holy Spirit among us for the forgiveness of sins;

through the ministry of the Church may God give you pardon and peace, and I absolve you from your sins in the name of the Father, and of the Son, and of the Holy Spirit.

The penitent answers: **Amen.**

PROCLAMATION OF PRAISE OF GOD AND DISMISSAL

After the absolution, the priest continues:

Give thanks to the Lord, for He is good.

The penitent concludes:

His mercy endures forever.

Then the priest dismisses the penitent who has been reconciled, saying:

The Lord has freed you from your sins. Go in peace.

Or:

May the Passion of Our Lord Jesus Christ,
the intercession of the Blessed Virgin Mary,
and of all the saints,
whatever good you do and suffering you endure,
heal your sins,
help you to grow in holiness,
and reward you with eternal life.
Go in peace.

APPENDIX B:
PRAYERS

ACT OF CONTRITION

O my God, I am heartily sorry for having offended You, and I detest all my sins because of Your just punishments, but most of all because they offend You, my God, Who are all-good and deserving of all my love. I firmly resolve, with the help of Your grace, to sin no more and to avoid the near occasions of sin. Amen.

ACT OF CONTRITION

My God, I am sorry for my sins with all my heart. In choosing to do wrong and failing to do good, I have sinned against You, Whom I should love above all things. I firmly intend, with Your help, to do penance, to sin no more, and to avoid whatever leads me to sin. Our Savior Jesus Christ suffered and died for us. In His name, my God, have mercy. Amen.

ACT OF CONTRITION

O my God, I am sorry for my sins because I have offended You. I know I should love You above all things. Help me to do penance, to do better, and to avoid anything that might lead me to sin. Amen.

PRAYER BEFORE CONFESSION

Receive my confession, O most loving and gracious Lord Jesus Christ, only hope for the salvation of my soul. Grant to me true contrition of soul, so that day and night I may by penance make satisfaction for my many sins.

Savior of the world, O good Jesus, Who gave Yourself to the death of the cross to save sinners, look upon me, most wretched of all sinners; have pity on me, and give me the light to know my sins, true sorrow for them, and a firm purpose of never committing them again.

O gracious Virgin Mary, Immaculate Mother of Jesus, I implore you to obtain for me by your powerful intercession these graces from your Divine Son.

Saint Joseph, pray for me.

PRAYER AFTER CONFESSION

O almighty and most merciful God, I give You thanks with all the powers of my soul for this and all other mercies, graces, and blessings bestowed on me, and prostrating myself at Your sacred feet, I offer myself to be henceforth forever Yours. Let nothing in life or death ever separate me from You! I renounce with my whole soul all my treasons against You, and all the abominations and sins of my past life. I renew my promises made in baptism, and from this moment I dedicate myself eternally to Your love and service. Grant that for the time to come, I may detest sin more than death itself and avoid all such occasions and companies as have unhappily brought me to it. This I resolve to do by the aid of Your divine grace, without which I can do nothing. Amen.

PSALM 51

A Psalm of David, when Nathan the prophet came to him, after he had gone in to Bathsheba.

APPENDIX B

Have mercy on me,
O God, according to Your steadfast love;
according to Your abundant mercy blot out my transgressions.
Wash me thoroughly from my iniquity
and cleanse me from my sin!
For I know my transgressions,
and my sin is ever before me.
Against You, You only, have I sinned,
and done that which is evil in Your sight,
so that You are justified in Your sentence
and blameless in Your judgment.
Behold, I was brought forth in iniquity,
and in sin did my mother conceive me.
Behold, You desire truth in the inward being;
therefore teach me wisdom in my secret heart.
Purge me with hyssop, and I shall be clean;
wash me, and I shall be whiter than snow.
Fill me with joy and gladness;
let the bones which You have broken rejoice.
Hide Your face from my sins,
and blot out all my iniquities.
Create in me a clean heart,
O God, and put a new and right spirit within me.
Cast me not away from Your presence
and take not Your Holy Spirit from me.
Restore to me the joy of Your salvation
and uphold me with a willing spirit.
Then I will teach transgressors Your ways,
and sinners will return to You.
Deliver me from blood guiltiness,

APPENDIX B

O God, God of my salvation,
and my tongue will sing aloud of Your deliverance.
O Lord, open my lips,
and my mouth shall show forth Your praise.
For You have no delight in sacrifice;
were I to give a burnt offering,
You would not be pleased.
The sacrifice acceptable to God is a broken spirit;
a broken and contrite heart,
O God, You will not despise.

THE CHAPLET OF DIVINE MERCY

Devotion to the Divine Mercy grew rapidly in the second half of the twentieth century, inspired by our Lord's revelations to Saint Faustina Kowalska (1905–1938). At the center of this devotion is the daily recitation of the Chaplet of Divine Mercy, at three o'clock in the afternoon, the hour of Jesus' death. The Chaplet of Mercy is recited using ordinary rosary beads of five decades.

Begin with the Our Father, Hail Mary, and Apostles' Creed:

Our Father, Who art in heaven, hallowed be Thy name; Thy kingdom come; Thy will be done, on earth as it is in heaven. Give us this day our daily bread; and forgive us our trespasses as we forgive those who trespass against us; and lead us not into temptation, but deliver us from evil. Amen.

Hail Mary, full of grace. The Lord is with thee. Blessed art thou amongst women, and blessed is the fruit of thy womb, Jesus. Holy Mary, Mother of God, pray for us sinners, now and at the hour of our death. Amen.

I believe in God, the Father Almighty, Creator of heaven and earth; and in Jesus Christ, His only Son, Our Lord, Who was conceived by the Holy Ghost, born of the Virgin Mary, suffered under Pontius Pilate, was crucified, died, and was buried. He descended into hell; the third day, He arose again from the dead; He ascended into heaven, sitteth at the right hand of God, the Father Almighty; from thence He shall come to judge the living and the dead. I believe in the Holy Spirit, the holy Catholic Church, the communion of saints, the forgiveness of sins, the resurrection of the body, and the life everlasting. Amen.

Then, on the large bead before each decade, pray:

Eternal Father,
I offer you the Body and Blood,
soul and divinity of Your dearly beloved Son,
Our Lord Jesus Christ,
in atonement for our sins
and those of the whole world.

On each of the ten small beads of each decade, say:

For the sake of His sorrowful passion,
have mercy on us and on the whole world.

At the end of each decade, repeat the following prayer three times:

Holy God,
Holy Mighty One,
Holy Immortal One,
have mercy on us
and on the whole world.

APPENDIX C:
EXAMINATION OF CONSCIENCE

The following examinations of conscience are reprinted, with permission, from the excellent *Handbook of Prayers*, edited by Father James Socias (Chicago: Midwest Theological Forum, 1995). You may use these as a guide, or come up with your own examination. Do whatever helps you to recall your sins. In the presence of God, calmly ask yourself what you have done with full knowledge and full consent against God's commandments.

THE FIRST COMMANDMENT
- Have I performed my duties toward God reluctantly or grudgingly?
- Did I neglect my prayer life? Did I recite my usual prayers?
- Did I receive holy Communion in the state of mortal sin or without the necessary preparation?
- Did I violate the one-hour Eucharistic fast?
- Did I fail to mention some grave sin in my previous confessions?
- Did I seriously believe in something superstitious or engage in a superstitious practice (palm-reading or fortune-telling for instance)?
- Did I seriously doubt a matter of faith?
- Did I put my faith in danger—without a good reason—by

reading a book, pamphlet, or magazine that contains material contrary to Catholic faith or morals?

- Did I endanger my faith by joining or attending meetings of organizations opposed to the Catholic faith (non-Catholic services, Freemasonry, New Age cults, or other religions)? Did I take part in one of its activities?
- Have I committed the sin of sacrilege (profanation of a sacred person, place, or thing)?

THE SECOND COMMANDMENT

- Did I fail to try my best to fulfill the promises and resolutions that I made to God?
- Did I take the name of God in vain? Did I make use of God's name mockingly, jokingly, angrily, or in any other irreverent manner?
- Did I make use of the Blessed Virgin Mary's name or another saint's name mockingly, jokingly, angrily, or in any other irreverent manner?
- Have I been a sponsor in baptism or participated actively in other ceremonies outside the Catholic Church?
- Did I tell a lie under oath?
- Did I break (private or public) vows?

THE THIRD COMMANDMENT

- Did I miss Mass on a Sunday or a holy day of obligation?
- Did I fail to dress appropriately for Mass?
- Have I, without sufficient reason, arrived at Mass so late that I failed to fulfill the Sunday or holy day of obligation?
- Did I allow myself to be distracted during Mass, by not paying attention, by looking around out of curiosity, etc.?

- Did I cause another to be distracted at Mass?
- Have I performed any work or business activity that would inhibit the worship due to God, the joy proper to the Lord's Day, or the appropriate relaxation of mind and body, on a Sunday or a holy day of obligation?
- Did I fail to generously help the Church in her necessities to the extent that I am able?
- Did I fail to fast or abstain on a day prescribed by the Church?

THE THIRD COMMANDMENT

For Parents

- Have I neglected to teach my children their prayers, send them to church, or give them a Christian education?
- Have I given them a bad example?
- Have I neglected to watch over my children; to monitor their companions, the books they read, the movies and TV shows they watch?
- Have I failed to see to it that my child made his first confession and first Communion?
- Have I failed to see to it that my children have received the sacrament of confirmation?

For Children

- Was I disobedient toward my parents?
- Did I neglect to help my parents when my help was needed?
- Did I treat my parents with little affection or respect?
- Did I react proudly when I was corrected by my parents?
- Did I have a disordered desire for independence?
- Did I do my chores?

THE FIFTH COMMANDMENT

- Did I easily get angry or lose my temper?
- Was I envious or jealous of others?
- Did I injure or take the life of anyone? Was I ever reckless in driving?
- Was I an occasion of sin for others by way of conversation; the telling of jokes religiously, racially, or sexually offensive; dressing; inviting somebody to attend certain shows; lending harmful books or magazines; helping someone to steal, etc.? Did I try to repair the scandal done?
- How many persons did I lead to sin? What sin or sins were involved?
- Did I neglect my health? Did I attempt to take my life?
- Have I mutilated myself or another?
- Did I get drunk or use prohibited drugs?
- Did I eat or drink more than a sufficient amount, allowing myself to get carried away by gluttony?
- Did I participate in any form of physical violence?
- Did I consent to or actively take part in direct sterilization (tubal ligation, vasectomy, etc.)? Do I realize that this will have a permanent effect on my married life and that I will have to answer to God for its consequences?
- Did I consent to, advise someone about, or actively take part in an abortion? Was I aware that the Church punishes with automatic excommunication those who procure and achieve abortion? Do I realize that this is a very grave crime?
- Did I cause harm to anyone with my words or actions?
- Did I desire revenge or harbor enmity, hatred, or ill feelings when someone offended me?
- Did I ask pardon whenever I offended anyone?

- Did I insult or offensively tease others?
- Did I quarrel with one of my brothers or sisters?

THE SIXTH AND NINTH COMMANDMENTS

- Did I willfully entertain impure thoughts?
- Did I consent to evil desires against the virtue of purity, even though I may not have carried them out? Were there any circumstances that aggravated the sin: affinity (relationship by marriage), consanguinity (blood relationship), either the married state or the consecration to God of a person involved?
- Did I engage in impure conversations? Did I start them?
- Did I look for fun in forms of entertainment that placed me in proximate occasions of sin, such as certain dances, movies, shows, or books with immoral content? Did I frequent houses of ill repute or keep bad company?
- Did I realize that I might already have been committing a sin by placing myself in a proximate occasion of sin, such as sharing a room with a person I find sexually attractive, or being alone with such a person in circumstances that could lead to sin?
- Did I fail to take care of those details of modesty and decency that are the safeguards of purity?
- Did I fail, before going to a show or reading a book, to find out its moral implications, so as not to put myself in immediate danger of sinning and in order to avoid distorting my conscience?
- Did I willfully look at an indecent picture or cast an immodest look upon myself or another? Did I willfully desire to commit such a sin?
- Did I lead others to sins of impurity or immodesty? What sins?
- Did I commit an impure act? By myself, through masturba-

tion (which is objectively a mortal sin)? With someone else? How many times? With someone of the same or opposite sex? Was there any circumstance of relationship (such as affinity) that could have given the sin special gravity? Did this illicit relationship result in pregnancy? Did I do anything to prevent or end that pregnancy?

- Do I have friendships that are habitual occasions of sexual sins? Am I prepared to end them?
- In courtship, is true love my fundamental reason for wanting to be with the other person? Do I live the constant and cheerful sacrifice of not putting the person I love in danger of sinning? Do I degrade human love by confusing it with selfishness or mere pleasure?
- Did I engage in acts such as "petting," "necking," passionate kisses, or prolonged embraces?

For Married People
- Did I, without serious reason, deprive my spouse of the marital right? Did I claim my own rights in a way that showed no concern for my spouse's state of mind or health? Did I betray conjugal fidelity in desire or in deed?
- Did I take "the pill" or use any other artificial birth-control device before or after new life had already been conceived?
- Did I, without grave reason, with the intention of avoiding conception, make use of marriage on only those days when offspring would not likely be engendered?
- Did I suggest to another person the use of birth-control pills or another artificial method of preventing pregnancy (like condoms)?
- Did I have a hand in contributing to the contraceptive mentality by my advice, jokes, or attitudes? (On abortion,

contraception, sterilization, etc., see also the Fifth Commandment.)

THE SEVENTH AND TENTH COMMANDMENTS

- Did I steal? How much money? Or how much was the object worth? Did I give it back or at least have the intention of doing so?
- Have I done or caused damage to another person's property? To what extent?
- Did I harm anyone by deception, fraud, or coercion in business contracts or transactions?
- Did I unnecessarily spend beyond my means? Do I spend too much money because of vanity or caprice?
- Do I give alms according to my capacity?
- Was I envious of my neighbor's goods?
- Did I neglect to pay my debts?
- Did I knowingly accept stolen goods?
- Did I desire to steal?
- Did I give in to laziness or love of comfort rather than diligently work or study?
- Was I greedy? Do I have an excessively materialistic view of life?

THE EIGHTH COMMANDMENT

- Did I tell lies? Did I repair any damage that may have resulted as a consequence of this?
- Have I unjustly or rashly accused others?
- Did I sin by detraction, that is, by telling the faults of another person without necessity?
- Did I sin by calumny, that is, by telling derogatory lies about another person?

- Did I engage in gossip, backbiting, or tale-telling?
- Did I reveal a secret without due cause?

SHORTER EXAMINATION OF CONSCIENCE

- When was my last good confession? Did I receive Communion or other sacraments while in the state of mortal sin? Did I intentionally fail to confess some mortal sin in my previous confession?
- Did I willfully and seriously doubt my faith, or put myself in danger of losing it by reading literature hostile to Catholic teachings or by getting involved with non-Catholic sects? Did I engage in superstitious activities, such as palm-reading, and fortune-telling?
- Did I take the name of God in vain? Did I curse or take a false oath? Did I use bad language?
- Did I miss Mass on a Sunday or a holy day of obligation through my own fault, without any serious reason? Did I fast and abstain on the prescribed days?
- Did I disobey my parents or lawful superiors in important matters?
- Was I selfish in how I treated others, especially my spouse, my brothers and sisters, my relatives, or my friends? Did I hatefully quarrel with anyone or desire revenge? Did I refuse to forgive? Did I cause physical injury or even death? Did I get drunk? Did I take illicit drugs? Did I consent to, advise someone about, or actively take part in an abortion?
- Did I willfully look at indecent pictures or watch immoral movies? Did I read immoral books or magazines? Did I engage in impure jokes or conversations? Did I willfully entertain impure thoughts or feelings? Did I commit impure acts, alone or with others? Did I take contraceptive or abortifa-

cient pills, or use other artificial means in order to prevent conception?

- Did I steal or damage another's property? How much was it worth? Have I made reparation for the damages done? Have I been honest in my business relations?
- Did I tell lies? Did I sin by slander? By detraction—telling unknown grave faults of others without necessity? Did I judge others rashly in serious matters? Have I tried to make restitution for any damage of reputation that I have caused?

If you remember other serious sins besides those indicated here, include them also in your confession.

SOURCES AND
REFERENCES

9 *"There is no more insidious way . . ."*: J. Pieper, *The Four Cardinal Virtues* (Notre Dame, Ind.: University of Notre Dame Press, 1966), 15.

14 *But in the tradition of Israel . . .* : See J. Klawans, *Impurity and Sin in Ancient Judaism* (New York: Oxford University Press, 2000); E. Mazza, *The Origins of the Eucharistic Prayer* (Collegeville, Minn.: Liturgical Press, 1995), 7; S. Lyonnet and L. Sabourin, *Sin, Redemption, and Sacrifice: A Biblical and Patristic Study* (Rome: Biblical Institute Press, 1970); S. Porubcan, *Sin in the Old Testament: A Soteriological Study* (Rome: Herder, 1963); B. F. Minchin, *Covenant and Sacrifice* (New York: Longmans, Green and Co., 1958).

Pope John Paul II stresses the need for restoring a proper sense of sin by drawing on Scripture: "There are good grounds for hoping that a healthy sense of sin will once again flourish. . . . This will be . . . illuminated by the biblical theology of the covenant . . ." On the distinctive nature and method of *biblical theology*, see A. Cardinal Bea, "Progress in the Interpretation of Sacred Scripture," *Theology Digest* 1.2 (Spring 1953): 71: "There has risen *biblical theology*, which is closely connected with exegesis. This science is not primarily concerned with finding arguments in Scripture for dogmatic truths. Rather, it aims at presenting, in a unified and systematic way, the origin and development of revealed doctrine in its successive stages. Thus, it takes individual truths out of their isolation and inserts them into a homogenous system, which is not something artificial, but rather a system willed by God Himself. This is perhaps the greatest progress exegesis has made in the course of centuries."

16 *He wants them to confess* . . . : See G. A. Anderson, "Punishment or Penance for Adam and Eve?" in *The Genesis of Perfection: Adam and Eve in Jewish and Christian Imagination* (Louisville: Westminster John Knox, 2001), 135–54.

19 *Take, for example, Leviticus 5:5–6* . . . : See H. Maccoby, *The Ritual Purity System and Its Place in Judaism* (New York: Cambridge University Press, 1999), 192: "For the function of the sin-offering (correctly so called) is . . . to expiate the sin of the offerer. This is why the culmination of the offering is the declaration . . . 'and he will be forgiven.'" Cf. J. Milgrom, *Leviticus 1–16* (New York: Doubleday, 1991); N. Kiuchi, *The Purification Offering in the Priestly Literature* (Sheffield: JSOT, 1981).

20 *Love means deeds* . . . : Saint Josemaría Escrivá, *The Way* (Manila: Sinag-Tala, 1982), no. 933.

22 *"Using a little imagination* . . ."*: G. J. Wenham, *The Book of Leviticus* (Grand Rapids, Mich.: Eerdmans, 1979), 52–55, 111. See G. J. Wenham, *Numbers: An Introduction and Commentary* (Downers Grove, Ill.: Inter-Varsity Press, 1981), 26–30: "The sheer bulk of ritual law in the Pentateuch indicates its importance to the biblical writers. . . . In short, if we do not understand the ritual system of a people, we do not understand what makes their society tick. . . . Moderns have a built-in antipathy to ritual and symbolic gestures. . . . Though such trends are more obvious among Protes-

tants, similar trends are discernible within Catholicism. . . . Very few would care for the expense, let alone the messiness, of Old Testament sacrifice. It is easy to sing . . . but to bring a whole bull, kill it, skin it, chop it up and then watch the whole lot burn on the altar, would be quite another matter. Yet this was precisely what someone who offered a burnt offering [Lev 1] was expected to do." Elsewhere, Wenham notes: "Leviticus in fact instructs the layman to kill his own animal, but in later times this right was restricted to the Levites, and later still to the priests alone" (p. 76). See also A. I. Baumgarten, ed., *Sacrifice in Religious Experience* (Leiden: E. J. Brill, 2002); R. T. Beckwith and M. J. Selman, *Sacrifice in the Bible* (Grand Rapids, Mich.: Baker Books, 1995); S. Sykes, ed., *Sacrifice and Redemption* (New York: Cambridge University Press, 1991); G. A. Anderson, *Sacrifice and Offerings in Ancient Israel* (Atlanta: Scholars Press, 1987); R. J. Daly, *The Origins of the Christian Doctrine of Sacrifice* (Philadelphia: Fortress Press, 1978); R. de Vaux, *Studies in Old Testament Sacrifice* (Cardiff: University of Wales Press, 1964); G. B. Gray, *Sacrifice in the Old Testament* (Oxford: Clarendon Press, 1925). On the ancient Israelite approach to guilt and innocence, suffering and penance, see G. Kwakkel, *According to My Righteousness: Upright Behaviour as Grounds for Deliverance* (Leiden: E. J. Brill, 2002); R. A. Weline, *Penitential Prayer in Second Temple Judaism: The Development of a Religious Institution* (Atlanta: Scholars Press, 1998); F. Linstrom, *Suffering and Sin: Interpretations of Illness in the Individual Complaint Psalms* (Stockholm: Almqvist & Wiksell, 1994).

23 *Lay people confessed their sins at least once a year . . .* : See J. Bonsirven, *Palestinian Judaism in the Time of Jesus* (New York: Holt, Rinehart and Winston, 1964), 116: "Penitence includes several acts. First, there should be a confession of sins, which ought to

precede any offering. It is also advisable to confess yearly on the Day of Atonement, together with the high priest, and several more times during one's life [*Tos. Yom Hakkippurim*, v, 14ff]. To be sincere, it ought to include a detailed admission of all the faults of which one has been guilty, and the promise to sin no more. If these two conditions are not fulfilled, it is false penitence and cannot lead to divine pardon. . . . [*Tos. Taan.*, 1, 8]. In addition, if you have wronged someone, you must repair the damage and try to be reconciled with him."

24 *We modern sinners could learn much . . . :* For a recent and very fruitful application of "speech act theory" to confession of sin and absolution (as "performative utterances," i.e., "binding and loosing"), see R. S. Briggs, *Words in Action: Speech Act Theory and Biblical Interpretation* (New York: T. & T. Clark, 2001), 217–55.

29 *He thus gave them a power exceeding . . . :* The power to "bind and loose," which Christ conferred upon the twelve apostles (Mt 18:18), is an integral part of the "keys of the kingdom," which Christ gave to Peter (Mt 16:17–19), both of which are related to the absolution of sins; see *CCC* 553: "The power to 'bind and loose' connotes the authority to absolve sins . . ." (see also *CCC* 979, 981, 1444).

31 *The term he uses for clergymen . . . :* See "*Presbyterorum Ordinis*" ("Decree on the Ministry and Life of Priests"), in A. Flannery, ed., *Vatican Council II: The Conciliar and Post Conciliar Documents* (Grand Rapids, Mich.: Eerdmans, 1992), 863–902. On the priestly role of the "elders" in Jas 5:14–16, see M. Miguens, *Church Ministries in New Testament Times* (Arlington, Va.: Christian Culture

Press, 1976), 78–79; see also R. A. Campbell, *The Elders: Seniority Within Earliest Christianity* (Edinburgh: T. & T. Clark, 1994), 234; and the ITC document, "The Priestly Ministry," in *International Theological Commission: Texts and Documents 1969–1985* (San Francisco: Ignatius Press, 1989), 45–63.

33 *Christians built their own synagogues . . . :* See L. M. White, "The Social Origins of Christian Architecture: Architectural Adaptation Among Pagans, Jews and Christians," *Harvard Theological Studies* 42 (Valley Forge, Pa.: Trinity Press International, 1996); G. F. Snyder, *Ante Pacem: Archaeological Evidence of Church Life Before Constantine* (Macon, Ga.: Mercer University Press, 1985).

33 *Some modern scholars say that parts . . . :* Mazza, *The Origins of the Eucharistic Prayer*, 40–41.

36 *I entreat you, beloved brethen . . . :* Saint Cyprian of Carthage, *The Lapsed* 29.

37 *The Egyptian scholar Origen . . . : Homilies on Leviticus* 2.4.5.

39 *"Justice and mercy . . ."*: Saint Thomas Aquinas, *Catena Aurea in Matthaeum* 5.5.

39 *"Mercy does not override justice . . ."*: P. Stravinskas, ed., *Catholic Encyclopedia* (Huntington, Ind.: Our Sunday Visitor, 1998), 666. See the encyclical letter by Pope John Paul II, *Dives in Misericordia: On the Mercy of God* (November 30, 1980); and S. Michalenko, "A Contribution to the Discussion on the Feast of Divine Mercy," in R. Stackpole, ed., *Divine Mercy: The Heart of the*

Gospel (Stockbridge, Mass.: John Paul II Institute of Divine Mercy, 1999), 128: "[A]ccording to Saint Thomas, Mercy is the first cause of all of creation, and Saint Bernard declares that Mercy is the *causa causissima causarum omnium.*" On the surpassing greatness of mercy as God's greatest attribute and very name, see Ex 33:17–23, and S. Hahn, *A Father Who Keeps His Promises: God's Covenant Love in Scripture* (Ann Arbor, Mich.: Servant Books, 1998), 159–60.

42–43 *In the early days, those who confessed serious sins . . . :* See J. A. Favazza, *The Order of Penitents: Historical Roots and Pastoral Future* (Collegeville, Minn.: Liturgical Press, 1988).

43 *The ordinary and "proper place . . .":* CIC, Can 964, § 1, 3; Pontifical Council for the Interpretation of Legislative Texts, *Responsa ad propositum dubium: de loco excipiendi sacramentales confessiones* (July 7, 1998): *AAS* 90 (1998), 711. Pope John Paul II, Motu Proprio *Misericordia Dei* (April 7, 2002).

44 *Yet the more things change . . . :* On the complex development of the sacrament of penance, see B. Poschmann, *Penance and the Anointing of the Sick* (New York: Herder and Herder, 1968), 5–219; P. Riga, *Sin and Penance: Insights into the Mystery of Salvation* (Milwaukee: Bruce Publishing, 1962), 78–122; O. D. Watkins, *A History of Penance,* 2 vols. (New York: Franklin, 1961); P. F. Palmer, *Sacraments and Forgiveness: History and Doctrinal Development of Penance, Extreme Unction, and Indulgences* (Westminster, Md.: Newman Press, 1959), 1–270; J. A. Spitzig, *Sacramental Penance in the Twelfth and Thirteenth Centuries* (Washington, D.C.: Catholic University of America Press, 1947).

On the formative influence of the medieval penitential books, see A. J. Minnis and P. Biller, eds., *Handling Sin: Confession in the*

Middle Ages (Rochester, N.Y.: York Medieval Press, 1998); H. Connolly, *The Irish Penitentials: Their Significance for the Sacrament of Penance Today* (Dublin: Four Courts Press, 1995); J. T. McNeill and H. M. Gamer, *Medieval Handbooks of Penance: A Translation of the Principal "Libri Poenitentiales"* (New York: Columbia University Press, 1990).

On the Catholic Church's doctrinal synthesis since Saint Thomas Aquinas, see J. M. T. Barton, *Penance and Absolution* (New York: Hawthorn, 1961); P. Galthier, *Sin and Penance* (New York: B. Herder, 1932); C. E. Schieler, *Theory and Practice of the Confessional* (New York: Benziger Brothers, 1905).

On the sacrament since Vatican II, see the apostolic exhortation by Pope John Paul II, *Reconciliatio et Paenitentia* (December 2, 1984); G. A. Kelly, ed., *The Sacrament of Penance in Our Time* (Boston: St. Paul Editions, 1976); cf. K. Osborne, *Reconciliation and Justification: The Sacrament and Its Theology* (New York: Paulist Press, 1990); J. Dallen, *The Reconciling Community: The Rite of Penance* (New York: Pueblo, 1986); M. K. Hellwig, *Sign of Reconciliation and Conversion: The Sacrament of Penance for Our Time* (Wilmington, Del.: Michael Glazer, 1984).

45 *Marriage was a covenant . . . :* See G. P. Hugenberger, *Marriage as a Covenant: A Study of Biblical Law and Ethics Governing Marriage* (Leiden: E. J. Brill, 1994), especially his exhaustive treatment of covenant-making and oath-swearing (pp. 168–279).

45 *"the liturgy of the renewal . . .":* Mazza, *The Origins of the Eucharistic Prayer,* 7.

45 *The Latin word for* oath . . . : See Pliny the Younger, *Epistle* 10.96; K. Hein, *Eucharist and Excommunication: A Study in Early*

Christian Doctrine and Discipline (Frankfurt: Peter Lang, 1973), 199–204; M. G. Kline, *By Oath Consigned: A Reinterpretation of the Covenant Signs of Circumcision and Baptism* (Grand Rapids, Mich.: Eerdmans, 1968), 79–81. The importance of oath-swearing in the covenantal praxis of the ancient Church reflects a similar phenomenon in ancient Israelite law and liturgy; see D. L. Magnetti's review of G. Giesen, *Die Wurzel "schworen,"* in *Journal of Biblical Literature* 103 (1984), 438: "The institution of the oath was of major importance in all facets of social, legal, and religious life in ancient Israel."

47 *The repentance has to be genuine . . . :* For a good treatment of the role of contrition in the teaching of Saint Thomas Aquinas, see H. J. M. Schoot, ed., *Tibi Soli Peccavi: Thomas Aquinas on Guilt and Forgiveness* (Leuven: Peeters, 1996); C. R. Meyer, *The Thomistic Concept of Justifying Contrition* (Mundelein, Ill.: Seminary Press, 1949).

49 *In times of dire emergency . . . :* See *CCC* 1483.

52 *The words of absolution are not . . . :* The absolving priest acts in the person of Christ. See *CCC* 1548–51.

54 *In the fourth century, Saint Basil said . . . : Rule* 288.

54 *In the same century, Saint Ambrose declared . . . : De poenitentiae,* II, ii, 12 (see I, ii, 6–7).

54 *Saint John Chrysostom . . . : On the Priesthood,* 3.5–6.

65 *Pope John Paul II said: "It is certainly . . .": Reconcilatio et Paenititentia,* 17.6.

65 *Pope John Paul II wrote: "Venial sin does not . . .":* Ibid., 17.9. He further explains: "Saint Augustine, among others, speaks of *letalia* or *mortifera crimina*, contrasting them with *venalia, levia* or *quotidiana*. The meaning which he gives to these adjectives was to influence the successive magisterium of the church. After him, it was Saint Thomas who was to formulate in the clearest possible terms the doctrine which became a constant in the church" (ibid., 17.8).

66 *Pope John Paul II taught: "It must not be forgotten . . .":* General Audience, March 11, 1984, n. 2.

67 *Said Pope John Paul II: "The confession of these sins . . .":* Ibid.

69 *The Hebrew actually repeats the word* die . . . : For a fuller explanation of the meaning of the Hebrew expression (*moth tamuth*), see S. Hahn, *First Comes Love: Finding Your Family in the Church and the Trinity* (New York: Doubleday, 2002), 66–75, 188–91; S. Sekine, *Transcendency and Symbols in the Old Testament* (New York: Walter de Gruyter, 1999), 240–42 ("Addendum [2]: On the contradiction surrounding dying").

70 *The greatest of the ancient Jewish commentators . . . :* Philo, *Legum Allegoriae* 1.105–108; cited by M. Kolarcik, *The Ambiguity of Death in the Book of Wisdom 1–6* (Rome: Pontifical Biblical Institute, 1991), 77.

71 *What is clear is that Adam faced a formidable, life-threatening force:* This section is adapted from Hahn, *First Comes Love,* 68–73, 187–88; idem, *A Father Who Keeps His Promises,* 65–71, 272–76. See C. Leget, *Living with God: Thomas Aquinas on the Relation Between*

Life on Earth and "Life" After Death (Leuven: Peeters, 1997), 117–18, 164–76, 265–66. See the document promulgated by the Congregation for the Doctrine of the Faith, *Christian Faith and Demonology* (Boston: St. Paul Books, 1975), 15–16: "This is why the Fathers of the Church, convinced from Scripture that Satan and the demons are the adversaries . . . have not failed to remind the faithful of their existence and activity. . . . In a broader and more forceful way, Saint Augustine showed him at work in the struggle of the 'two cities'. . . . In the society of sinners he saw a mystical 'body' of the devil, and this idea recurs later in Saint Gregory the Great's *Moralia in Job*" (citing *De Civitate Dei* XI, 9; *PL* 34.441–41; *PL* 76, 694, 705, 722).

73 *Pope Pius XI wrote . . . :* "On the Church and the Third Reich," in *Mit Brennender Sorge* (March 14, 1937); he continues: "It is the loss of grace, and therefore of eternal life, which everybody must—with the assistance of grace, penance, resistance, and moral effort—repress and conquer." On the notion of original sin as the "death of the soul" through the "loss of divine life," see C. Schonborn, *Loving the Church* (San Francisco: Ignatius Press, 1998), 68–69: "Original sin is not a positive quality inherited by each man from his forefathers, but rather the lack of a quality that he should have inherited. . . . One can interpret original sin, therefore, as the initial state of not belonging to the People of God." See M. J. Scheeben, *The Mysteries of Christianity* (St. Louis: Herder, 1946), 295–310; C. Belmonte, ed., *Faith Seeking Understanding: A Complete Course of Theology*, vol. 1 (Manila: Studium Theologiae Foundation, 1993), 248–51; *DS* 1512–13.

74 *The Law of (Moral) Gravity:* See S. Pinckaers, *Morality: The Catholic View* (South Bend, Ind.: St. Augustine's Press, 2001); idem,

SOURCES AND REFERENCES

The Sources of Christian Ethics (Washington, D.C.: Catholic University of America Press, 1995); R. Cessario, *Introduction to Moral Theology* (Washington, D.C.: Catholic University of America Press, 2001).

77 *Sacramental Confection . . . : The Confessions of St. Augustine* (New York: Doubleday 1960), 69–76.

83 *Theologians call it* concupiscence . . . : Taken from the "Glossary and Index Analyticus," in *Catechism of the Catholic Church* (Washington, D.C.: USCC, 2000), 871–72. See J. J. Hugo, *St. Augustine on Nature, Sex, and Marriage* (Chicago: Scepter Press, 1969), 52–78; Belmonte, *Faith Seeking Understanding,* 251.

85 *Punished by Pleasure:* See J. Gildea, trans., *Source Book of Self-Discipline: A Synthesis of* "Moralia in Job" *by Gregory the Great (A Translation of Peter of Waltham's* "Remediarium Conversorum"*)* (New York: Peter Lang, 1991), 47–56, 129–46, 152–60, 173, 193–200; L. E. Vaage and V. Wimbush, *Asceticism and the New Testament* (New York: Routledge, 1999); E. A. Clark, *Reading Renunciation: Asceticism and Scripture in Early Christianity* (Princeton, N.J.: Princeton University Press, 1999); T. M. Shaw, *The Burden of the Flesh: Fasting and Sexuality in Early Christianity* (Minneapolis: Fortress Press, 1998). For an outstanding treatment of this emphasis in Saint Gregory's moral and spiritual theology, see C. Straw, *Gregory the Great: Perfection in Imperfection* (Los Angeles: University of California Press, 1988). Cf. C. S. Lewis, *The Allegory of Love: A Study in Medieval Tradition* (London: Oxford University Press, 1959), 14–23.

88 *Saint Thomas Aquinas explains . . . : Summa Theologica* I. 1. 10 ad 3. Saint Thomas Aquinas interprets God's wrath as figurative

yet real, that is, as an anthropomorphic expression that describes how God's holy and just love is experienced by an impenitent sinner who refuses His mercy. See F. J. de Grijs, "Thomas Aquinas on *Ira* as a Divine Metaphor," in Schoot, *Tibi Soli Peccavi*, 19–46; Luigi Cardinal Ciappi, *The Heart of Christ: The Center of the Mystery of Salvation* (Rome: CDC Publishers, 1983), 26–30. Cf. J. I. Packer, *Knowing God* (Downers Grove, Ill.: Inter-Varsity Press, 1973), 139, who advocates the common evangelical Protestant view of the wrath of God as an "emotional attitude . . . of hatred of irreligion."

89 *God's anger has been defined as . . . :* de Grijs, "Thomas Aquinas on *Ira* as a Divine Metaphor," 44. He adds, "[T]hat which is signified in the metaphor of the anger of God, should become somewhat clearer: namely, the Triune God, Who does not allow Himself to be held in contempt, is a God of love Whose kingdom is not a nursery" (p. 45). He summarizes Saint Thomas's careful treatment of the 168 Old Testament passages that speak of God's wrath: "It is not said of God in a proper sense, because it implies a passion and therefore a bodily component and reactivity" (p. 29). He thus concludes: "Scripture's speaking of God's *iustitia* [justice] and *misericordia* [mercy] can only be understood as being rooted in the *amor Dei* [love of God] and as elaborations of what is meant by *amor Dei* . . . Scripture does speak in truth of God's anger and vengeance, but He punishes *ex animi tranquillitate*: God never loses His temper" (pp. 33–34).

95 *Thus, we come to the vocabulary . . . :* For the various "models of the atonement," see R. Nicole, "The Nature of Redemption," in *Standing Forth: The Collected Writings of Roger Nicole* (Roshire, U.K.: Focus, 2002), 245–82; J. B. Green and M. D.

Baker, *Recovering the Scandal of the Cross: Atonement in New Testament and Contemporary Contexts* (Downers Grove, Ill.: Inter-Varsity Press, 2000). For a profound treatment of Paul's use of "economic" terms in describing salvation, interpreted in the light of cultic worship and ancient "temple economies" (in Judaea and the Greco-Roman world), see D. Georgi, "Is There Justification in Money? A Historical and Theological Meditation on the Financial Aspects of Justification by Christ," in *Remembering the Poor: The History of Paul's Collection for Jerusalem* (Nashville: Abingdon Press, 1992), 141–65. See also Hahn, *First Comes Love*, 82–94.

99 *But, according to the logic of the covenant* . . . : See Ciappi, *The Heart of Christ*, 234–35: "The mystery of Redemption is essentially and principally a mystery of love. The Bible, the Fathers of the Church, and Catholic theology in general tell us that Jesus Christ has made infinite satisfaction for all the sins of mankind, meriting an infinite treasure of expiation, not because He was made the object of the vindictive hatred of God the Father . . . but because He freely immolated Himself on the altar of the Cross, as the Head of a new humanity, driven on by His immense love: 'Christ, suffering in a loving and obedient spirit, offered more to God than was demanded in recompense for all the sins of mankind' " (citing Thomas Aquinas, *Summa Theologica* III, 48.2) Elsewhere, Aquinas notes: "God desired to manifest His infinite mercy in such a way that His justice should be in no way compromised" (*III Sent., Dist. I, 1, 2*, cited by Ciappi, p. 40). For recent magisterial teachings that affirm "covenant representation" and "vicarious satisfaction," but not "penal substitution," see "Select Questions on Christology" in *International Theological Commission Documents*, 200–202: "What was traditionally called 'vicarious expiation' must be understood, transformed, and raised to the height of a 'Trinitarian event'. . . . Through the concept of substitu-

tion, the stress falls on the fact that Christ takes on the condition of sinners. This is not to say that God punished or condemned Christ in our stead, a theory erroneously advanced by many authors, Reformed theologians in particular." Recently, a growing number of evangelical Protestants are drawing very similar conclusions; see M. J. Gorman, *Cruciformity: Paul's Narrative Spirituality of the Cross* (Grand Rapids, Mich.: Eerdmans, 2001); J. R. Wilson, *God So Loved the World* (Grand Rapids, Mich.: Baker Books, 2001).

100 *The sacraments are now the means . . . :* On the derivation of the Church's sacraments from Christ's saving passion, see Saint Thomas Aquinas's commentary on the Sentences (*IV Sent.*, d. 18 q. 1a. 1 qc. 1): "The door of the kingdom is closed to us through sin. . . . Thus, the power by which such an obstacle to entrance into the kingdom is removed is called a key. . . . This power is in the most Holy Trinity by authority, but this power was in Christ's humanity for the removal of this obstacle through the merit of his passion. . . . Now the sacraments flowed from the side of Christ sleeping on the cross, by which the Church was created. For this reason the very efficacy of the passion remains in the sacraments of the Church. It is on this account that, in the ministers of the Church, who are the dispensers of the sacraments, a certain power remains for the removal of the aforementioned obstacle. And this power is not proper to the ministers, but it is the divine power from the passion of Christ. This power is metaphorically called the key of the Church, which is the key of ministry." For Saint Thomas Aquinas, our sin is overcome—in justice—by Christ's love, like ice is overcome—in nature—by the sun's warmth.

102 *As Saint Athanasius declared . . . : De Incarnatione* 54, 3: *PG* 25, 192B; see J. Gross, *The Divinization of the Christian According to*

the Greek Fathers (Anaheim, Calif.: A & C Publishers, 2002); J. D. Finch, "Sanctity as Participation in the Divine Nature According to the Ante-Nicene Eastern Fathers, Considered in the Light of Palamism" (Ph.D. diss., Drew University, 2002); *CCC* 460.

108 *The pharisees observed these traditions . . . :* See T. Kazen, *Jesus and Purity "Halakhah": Was Jesus Indifferent to Impurity?* (Stockholm: Almqvist & Wiksell, 2002); J. Neusner, *The Rabbinic Traditions About the Pharisees Before 70* (Lanham, Md.: University Press of America, 1999), 291–94. See also Saint Thomas Aquinas, *Summa Theologica* I–II: 102, 5, 4: "The figurative reason for the different kinds of ritual impurity was that each signified different kinds of sin. The uncleanness of a corpse signified the uncleanness of sin, which is the death of the soul. The uncleanness of leprosy signified heretical doctrine, since it is contagious, like leprosy . . ."

112 *The old man then does something remarkable:* See K. Bailey, *The Cross and the Prodigal: The 15th Chapter of Luke, Seen Through the Eyes of Middle Eastern Peasants* (St. Louis: Concordia, 1973), 54–61.

112 *The third-century commentator Origen . . . :* Origen, *Homilies on Luke* (Washington, D.C.: Catholic University of America Press, 1996), 215.

116 *This is the rhetoric of slavery, not sonship.:* See Pope John Paul II, *Crossing the Threshold of Hope* (New York: Alfred A. Knopf, 1994), 227–28: "One might think—and there is no lack of evidence to this effect—that Hegel's paradigm of the master and the servant is more present in people's consciousness today than is wisdom, whose origin lies in the filial fear of God. . . . The only

force capable of effectively counteracting this philosophy is found in the Gospel of Christ, in which the paradigm of master-slave is radically transformed into the paradigm of *father-son. The father-son paradigm is ageless.* It is older than human history. The 'rays of fatherhood' contained in this formulation belong to the Trinitarian Mystery of God Himself, which shines forth from Him, illuminating man and his history. . . . *Original sin attempts, then, to abolish fatherhood* . . . , placing in doubt the truth about God Who is Love and leaving man only with a sense of the master-slave relationship."

122 *The spiritual writer Father John Hugo . . . :* J. J. Hugo, *Your Ways Are Not My Ways* (Pittsburgh: Encounter with Silence, 1984), 113. See Saint Augustine, *De Doctrina Christiana* 4: "Suppose, then, we were wanderers in a strange country, and could not live happily away from our fatherland, and that we felt wretched in our wandering, and wishing to put an end to our misery, determined to return home. We find, however, that we must make use of some mode of travel, either by land or water, in order to reach that fatherland where our enjoyment will commence. But the beauty of the country through which we pass, and the very pleasure of the motion, charm our hearts, and turning these things which we ought to use into objects of enjoyment, we become unwilling to hasten the end of our journey; and becoming engrossed . . . our thoughts are diverted from that home whose delights would make us truly happy. Such is a picture of our condition in this life of mortality. We have wandered far from God; and if we wish to return to our Father's home, this world must be used, not enjoyed . . . that is, by means of what is material and temporary we may lay hold of that which is spiritual and eternal."

124 *That is one reason why God commanded them to sacrifice . . . :* See M. Aberbach and L. Smolar, "The Golden Calf Episode in

Post-Biblical Judaism," *Hebrew Union College Annual* 39 (1968): 91–116; P. C. Bori, *The Golden Calf and the Origins of the Anti-Jewish Controversy* (Atlanta: Scholars Press, 1990); S. W. Hahn, "Kinship by Covenant: A Biblical Theological Study of Covenant Types and Texts in the Old and New Testaments" (Ph.D. diss., Marquette University; Ann Arbor, Mich.: UMI, 1995), 44–51; Saint Thomas Aquinas, *Summa Theologica* I–II, 102, 3: "Thus, another reason is given for the sacrificial ceremonies, that is, they served to withdraw the people from offering sacrifices to idols. That is the reason why the precepts that required animal sacrifice were not given to the Jewish people until after they fell into idolatry by adoring the golden calf . . ."

127 *As Egyptian slavery was a type of original sin . . .* : See J. Corbon, *Path to Freedom: Christian Experiences and the Bible* (New York: Sheed and Ward, 1969), 172: "The Babylonian Captivity is analogous to the period of bondage in Egypt. Historically, it is simply a repetition by an Eastern power of the pattern established by a Western power. But there is a significant theological difference. During the captivity in Egypt the People of God was still amorphous. In leaving Egypt it leaves the first slavery . . . just as we, through baptism, are delivered from the bondage of original sin. But in the case of the Babylonian Captivity, Israel falls into bondage by its own fault just as we are enslaved by our own, personal sin."

129 *Like the sacrifice of Egypt's sacred animals . . .* : On the notion of "normative inversion," as applied to God's purpose in requiring Israel to sacrifice precisely those animals which Egyptians venerated or worshiped, see J. Assmann, *Moses the Egyptian* (Cambridge, Mass.: Harvard University Press, 1997), 31ff.; S. Benin,

211

The Footprints of God (Albany, N.Y.: SUNY Press, 1993); Hahn, *A Father Who Keeps His Promises*, 282–84.

139 *More than 61 percent of American . . . :* A. Spake, "Super Size America," *U.S. News & World Report* (Aug. 19, 2002, cover story); see also N. Hellmich, "Obesity in America Is Worse than Ever," *USA Today* (Oct. 9, 2002), page 1A.

142 *Indeed, the Church teaches . . . :* Vatican II, *Gaudium et Spes*, 24.

142 *Consider the inner life of the Trinity:* See Pope John Paul II, *Letter to Families* (Boston: St. Paul Books, 1994); K. Hahn, "Triune Family: Life-Giving Lovers and Life-Loving Givers" in *Life-Giving Love: Embracing God's Beautiful Design for Marriage* (Ann Arbor, Mich.: Charis, 2002), 31–47; S. Hahn, *First Comes Love*, 120–24.

143 *"the only creature on earth . . .":* Vatican II, *Gaudium et Spes*, 24.

150 *A regular confessor can be like a family physician . . . :* On the risk of frequently changing confessors, see Saint Francis de Sales, *Introduction to the Devout Life*, Part II, ch. xix.

150 *But, as a friend of mine put it . . . :* M. Aquilina, "How to Find a Regular Confessor," *New Convenant* (Sept. 1996), 8.

154 *Going to confession is hard . . . :* D. Day, *The Long Loneliness* (New York: Harper & Row, 1952), 9–12.

160 *Rabbi Nahum Sarna, echoing the ancient rabbis . . . :* N. Sarna, *Understanding Genesis: The Heritage of Biblical Israel* (New York:

Schocken, 1966), 150–51. See E. E. Urbach, *The Sages: Their Concepts and Beliefs* (Jerusalem: Magnes Press, 1979), 483–511; A. Marmorstein, *The Doctrine of Merits in Old Rabbinical Literature* (New York: KTAV, 1968); G. F. Moore, *Judaism* (Cambridge, Mass.: Harvard University Press, 1927), I, 535–45. Cf. *CCC* 1476–77.

162 *Half of the penitents . . . :* W. Fowlie, *Journal of Rehearsals: A Memoir* (Durham, N.C.: Duke University Press, 1977), 77–78.

163–64 *Saint Augustine warns us . . . : Tractate on the First Epistle of John* 1.6.

166 "Go in peace": Final blessing, rite of reconciliation.

168 *The Protestant reformer Martin Luther . . . :* "The Pagan Servitude of the Church," in J. Dillenberger, ed., *Martin Luther: Selections from His Writings* (New York: Doubleday, 1961), 319, 357.

168–69 *C. S. Lewis felt the attraction . . . :* R. L. Green and W. Hooper, *C. S. Lewis: A Biography* (New York: Harcourt, Brace, Jovanovich, 1974), 198.

172 *In ancient Israel, a "jubilee year" . . . :* See R. North, *Sociology of the Biblical Jubilee* (Rome: Pontifical Biblical Institute, 1954); idem, *The Biblical Jubilee . . . After Fifty Years* (Rome: Biblical Institute Press, 2000).

173 *"Mercy wishes that you be merciful . . ."*: Saint Leo the Great, Homily 95.7. See the encyclical letter by Pope John Paul II, *Dives in Misericordia* (November 30, 1980), II.4: "In this way, mercy is in a certain sense contrasted with God's justice, and in